Blood in the Bayou

A Record of the Operations and Blessed Techniques

Of a Doctor of Conjure-Work

by

Docteur Sureaux

Blood in the Bayou

A Record of the Operations and Blessed Techniques
Of a Doctor of Conjure-Work

by

Docteur Sureaux

First Edition © **2015**

by

Pendraig Publishing

All Rights Reserved

No part of this publication may be reproduced, stored in a retrieval system or transmitted in any form or by any means, electronic, mechanical, photocopying, recording or otherwise without the prior written permission of the copyright holder, except for brief quotation in a review.

Cover art, interior typeset, and layout
by Christopher Graham

Pendraig Publishing
Los Angeles, CA **91040**
www.pendraigpublishing.com
Printed in the United States of America

ISBN: 978-1-936922-78-9

Contents

part I:
back to the roots
or
the bayou country

part II:
dream-visions
and
serpent weave

part III:
spirit-talking, the invisible work,
and the great darkness

part IV:
charms, tricks, and lores

Part I:
Back to the Roots, or The Bayou Country

"Well there was a time not long ago
When you showed me what was down below,
But you don't show me that anymore, do ya?
Do you remember when I moved in you?
And the holy dove, She was moving too;
And every breath we drew was Hallelujah..."
                            -Leonard Cohen

I. Rude Heathen Catholicism and the Religion of Spirits

I wish there was some way I could share what I've experienced in my life with you, but all I can do is type out some words that I hope will suffice. These words are a great distance from the experiences themselves; the sights, the sounds, the smells, the feelings and the deep longing and pleasure and pain that make up any life. This life began almost **50** years ago in South Louisiana. My first **19** years were spent between my hometown of Vacherie, Louisiana, and New Orleans, and often enough in the country of Iberville, Assumption, and Saint Martin Parishes.

Some visions from my first years remain. I remember sitting at the bedside of my great-grandmother Odette, and seeing the statues of saints and the Virgin Mother on her bed stand, surrounded by countless translucent brown bottles of medicine, with a rosary winding about them. I remember telling her that I was three years old, and I know that's what I was doing, because in my mind's eye, I see my small hand holding up three fingers in front of her wrinkled, smiling face.

The house she lived in was a small wood-framed thing, in the yard near the home of her son, my grandfather, Pierre. Families lived close together back then, and took care of their elderly members. These people - my father's people - were Catholics, and much to the horror of the Protestants who dwelled here and there up and down the Bayou country, they were the equivalent of heathen polytheists - worshipers of Mary and the various saints. The logic is quite simple; Mary and the Saints are in heaven, closer to God. Mary, the mother of Jesus, has his ear, because Jesus is his Mother's son, even in the glory of eternity. To ask the saints and the Mother for help interceding with God and the heavenly host only makes sense to Catholic people. And unlike their protestant neighbors, nothing holds Catholics back from asking Jim Beam or Jack Daniels, or even the Old Milwaukee Brewery for a little comfort and aid, when in need.

These people knew how to live life. They smiled more, and had parties more, and cooked more and better - and they knew who needed candles and prayers for safe journeys - that would be Saint Michael. If you had a desperate situation or a hopeless case, Saint Jude would be your man. Pregnant women and even sterile women could expect Saint Anthony to help them - and he also helped to find lost things. They named me after him, and made him my patron.

If it turned out that the saints weren't listening when you had an especially pressing need, you could always take the laminated image of them, or the small card bearing their image (which was normally prominently displayed) and turn it backwards, hiding it behind books or candles or the pictures of other saints. This shaming would certainly get the attention of the Saint, and give him some motivation to help you out. Most people might find that an odd practice, but I read some years later that Catholics in Italy have gone further, in some small villages: they would take the statue of their patron saint out of the village and put him upside down in the mud of a river, only restoring him to his church or shrine when he helped them to resolve their situation.

Most Christians (and perhaps even some Catholics from other parts of the world) might think this presumptuous on the parts of men and women, but another author I read pointed out that in the rudest, most ancient forms of spirit-worship, spirits are often menaced by shamans to get their obedience or help. The author believed (and I am inclined to agree) that some vestigial aspect of this ancient sort of spirit-cajoling remains operative in the souls of these Heathen Catholics.

Those Heathen Catholics are my roots and origins. I am still technically a member of the Holy Roman Church. I do not consider myself a member, but Mother Church doesn't release people who are united to her, ever. There is no form to fill out requesting a release. To them, I'm a fallen away Catholic, an apostate Catholic, corrupted and eaten up with heresy, apostasy, and sorcery. And that's fine. In some parts of the world - like the one that I came from - that makes me a better Catholic, in a way. I do not attend masses nor believe in the myths and stories of the bible or the church, but I respect its aesthetic and its more celebratory traditions. I lament the lame social doctrines promulgated by the leadership of the Catholic church, but then, so do most of my Catholic relatives, so I'm clean on that point again.

I don't know about "God", nor saints, nor angels. I know about spirits. I know that spirits exist; some very powerful, some less so, but all mysterious and capable of bringing about changes in this world. Some are helpful to man. Some are harmful. Some don't care. Some are beyond our comprehension. All can take on countless forms when they appear to a human's mind or eyes. The more powerful they are, the more forms they can take. And I know a secret about the Catholic Church that even most Catholics don't know.

Without realizing it, the Catholic Church was responsible for the spread of one of the world's most ancient religions: the animistic and polytheistic religions of West Africa. If you look at it from another angle, whatever was Catholic changed forever when slaves arrived in the New World aboard Portuguese, French, and Spanish ships; these slaves carried with them the essence of the spirit-worship of their homelands, and the names and rituals of those great powers, and they didn't give them up. At the hands of priests and European slave-owners living on plantations along the Mississippi, they were "converted" to Catholicism, but the conversion wasn't a one-way road. Ironically, the conversion was backwards.

The slaves looked upon the icons of saints and heard their holy stories, and they looked upon the icons of the Virgin Mother, and saw their own spirits and Gods gazing back at them. By necessity, the ancient powers were gradually worshiped through the saints and the Mother of God, and the syncretism that we today call Vodou was born. Also born from this strange coterie was Santeria and other faiths. Those old blacks knew something that their owners and the priests couldn't begin to fathom - that the Lwa, the ancient and ever-living powers, didn't care what image or name their worshipers were using to call them. Spirits see deeper than that. They see better than that. Spirits are shape-shifters, after all. They change their skins like we change our clothes.

And spirits have long memories, and they have powers of far, far hearing. Once Old Man Legba hears that "Saint Peter" is what his children are calling him, Old Man Legba will be happy to become a new sort of key-holder. And forever after that, when he hears Peter's name being called anywhere, he might be paying attention.

Catholicism was changed, forever. It was, as I say, "spiritized"; the church is now haunted by powers it never had before - and perhaps, because of that, it has gained new powers to help people (or harm them) that it never had before. A new family of spiritual powers now inhabit it, surround it, thanks to the influx of dark flesh and massive, primal spiritual power from West Africa. Today, an old churchman in Belgium might say his prayers to St. Peter or to Mary herself, and gain his heart's desire, without considering that Legba or Erzulie Dantor was listening. The secret lives of spirits, and the way they interact with us, is a hidden thing to most. But a conjure-man or woman, a sorcerer, has to know. They have to pay attention, and most of all, they have to be flexible.

No quality defines the mind of a cunning man or woman, a real sorcerer, more than flexibility. Life is water, not stone- and the spirit-world is of a strange, quicksilver substance that makes even earthly water seem stone-like. The unseen world and its powers- and the sum-total of those powers- are practically incomprehensible to a mind that tries to make sense out of them. A sorcerer is like a spirit in some ways, more than other men or woman- a sorcerer is a shape-shifter, too. And only a flexible mind can shift its shape and contents and feelings around enough to deal with the unseen, or even with tough situations in this life. In the quicksilver mystery of spirit, there's nothing to hold onto. But there is power to be obtained.

When you stop trying to make it all make sense, and you just accept whatever comes, you start to gain power, start to gain insight. We don't have to "figure it all out" for it to have power or to work. Our job isn't to take on more than we can; our job is to be present with what we have, to be attentive, respectful, and even brave sometimes. Trust in the sacred powers comes from that healthy attitude of humility for what we can't understand.

I float free in trust in spiritual forces. What is most important is taken care of - my family. My unseen family comes to visit me, too, often after I burn enough sweetgrass or rattle enough for them, to make them come tickling up my spine and filling my chest. Together, we go forward to whatever dreams may come.

I am a Maître de Carrefour, a master of crossroads. Left? Right? Forward? Back? Or just drifting in the center, in all possibility? I drift in the center with the Hibou, with the unshelled turtle, with the old lady who lost her eyes, with the mouse that promised to care for my youngest daughter, with the swamp devils that took care of me as a boy running with dirty feet and skinned knees. Our center is everywhere, and it is spreading out further and further, until even stars are in our midst.

I grew up surrounded by spirits, some masked as saints, others not even caring to hide behind that easy disguise. Some of them were red-skinned, with big bulbous heads and fiddles, others were devil-like, skittering off behind trees and thick undergrowth. Some were animal-like. Some were just a pressure on your skin in bed at night, a hand holding your arm which made you freeze in fear in your own bed. A young mind like mine was scared of them half the time, and in wonder the other half.

The young, the "holy little ones", are blessed to have a lot of natural interactions with spiritual powers. Then, the forgetfulness comes. I was fortunate; I didn't forget a lot of what I saw. I remember seeing the world like it was on fire - beds, tables, armoires dancing with odd tongues of light, with misty apparitions floating in mid-air in the rooms. And I never forgot it.

I'm not a practitioner of the Vodou religion, but it feels natural to me. I'm not afraid of it (except when I think I need to be) and I'm not uncomfortable with it. I don't worship spirits in the extremely complicated (and beautiful) way they do; but I do have interactions with spirits, and some of them are likely the same spirits. I'm going to talk at length about my own way of power, soon enough. It's enough to understand that these powers - whatever they are - are real and present in all places where I'm from, and even beyond that. The real religion of this world is hidden. It hides because people decide that things have to be one way, and they go rigid, while fluid spirits slide between their fingers and care little over their fantasies.

II. Mother Swamp, Sultan Orleans

You can't separate Southern Louisiana cultures like the Cajuns or Creoles, nor their Catholicism, nor American Vodou even, from the landscape. South Louisiana is swampy, with countless miles of beautiful wetlands, spillways, and swamps. Now, to be fair, it looks better in pictures, because when you get out to the swamps, heat and mosquitoes and snakes become an issue. This doesn't take away its beauty, nor its spiritual power - because everything has spiritual power, including mosquitoes and snakes, and heat and moisture. All together, swamps themselves are wombs; teeming with life and rot and more life.

All ancient people that I know of look upon the land that they live on as a mother. It only makes sense on multiple levels; the earth is yielding to the seed and plow, and brings forth new life from within itself. But for those who don't grow their food in that way, the earth still gives - berries, fruits, and animals. The earth opens up and takes back everything that falls dead or is left out long enough and unattended, even mighty cities. The earth is what we're made of - this flesh of ours, in all its different shades of clay, can be found reflected back from the ground, somewhere; there is darkest mud, whitest dirt and sand, reddish clay, and yellowish clay. The elements of these bodies are all right there in the ground under our feet. We've gotten loose for a while, but we'll all go back down, one day.

And this is where most people stop when it comes to ecological pondering regarding the relationship of humans to the land. But a sorcerer goes further - the land itself, and these swamps, are not just biomass. They are the very presence of powerful spirits. All my life, the great "wise" people of the occult world and the deep ecology world have preached how all things are united, all are one, and many other wonderful teachings. But what none of them ever told me was what I had to uncover myself - that the consequences of "oneness" are very practical, not lofty and abstract. When you feel the mud ooze between your toes, hear the crickets, feel the humidity, and smell the rot, you are encountering spirits, full blown spirits.

These sensory experiences aren't "just" sensory experiences. They are the words and bodies and presence of spirits.

The Mother-Land, the Mother-Swamp, is a person; she is a non-human person, with her own intentions, memories, and powers. She is ancient beyond ancient, mother to all living. Stories and myths about her have been born from human minds in every age, and today, her final resting place in southern civilization is in any shrine where a statue of the Virgin Mary stands, or on any novena-card or plastic image of Mary. And she doesn't care about all the stories of the past, nor the prayers of the present. If you want to give her a Greek dress and call her Barley Mother, fine. If you want to pray to her as the mother of Jesus, or the Mother of Roots, that's fine, too.

Her concern is not names or myths, but the healthful presence and well-being of her many children. She thinks of us in terms of a group, a population; sometimes she stands by while many die, but she receives them nonetheless; sometimes she actively protects and nurtures - it's for her mystery to say. And she's present to us all, right now, ageless and new. She, like all spirits, cannot be closed in by religion or imagination. And the cunning Conjure-man or Cunning Woman can receive of that Mother a power to lay tricks and make magic that exceeds any in the world, if they know the way.

The swamplands of Louisiana are mother-lands to many cultures, from the earliest Natives who were always here, to the cultures of my own people, who came here on boats or on foot from Nova Scotia, or on boats from France and Spain. I'm a native of this place, too - a native son just like any red-skinned man or woman. There was a time when white-skins weren't natives, but intruders and wanderers. But now, white-skins have buried generations of their kin in this land, and eaten the food of this place, eaten the animals of this place, mingled their blood with the red natives of this place, and become part of this place.

The religions of the white people were changed by this place. Their lifestyles were changed by this place. Nature, and this land, is a house of transformations and shape-shifting, a great magic all its own, greater than even human empires. Greater than the far reaches of space, or the deep oceans, all is contained in the weird magic of things. This is how a sorcerer considers it - we are all changing, individually, as cultures, as a society, as human beings.

We're being warped like wood in the humid swamp, like dead leaves rotting in the stagnant water. We're all living and dying and changing, all the time. What looks so stable to us right now is just another arc in the mighty changeful power. We're all in the hands of greater powers and changes; I call that "fate", and it gives me a reason to stop sometimes, sit back, and be whoever I happen to be, however I happen to be, and enjoy the show more, instead of getting upset about it.

I've traveled around a bit. A person from Louisiana who never travels can't really understand just how unique Louisiana is, compared to the other lower 48 states. "Normal" in Louisiana is out of step with "normal" anywhere else.

"Normal" for me is the deep south of the Acadiana Parishes, with Spanish moss and deep, swampy land, all filled with a phantasmagoria of characters including the Cajun people - who are my people - and their habit of boiling crawfish that they dragged out of the murky water and enjoying them so spiced up that your lips swell up and your eyes water. Cheap beer and Blues and Zydeco music are everywhere a person cares to look or listen. Creoles and black people with their overdressed congregations on Sundays, howling away with their haunting and over-hopeful gospel hymns; Native Americans with their casinos; Pentecostals getting carried away and babbling; Baptists making asses of themselves in the news by preaching against everything that is fun and good in this world: my birth-home is a place like no other.

There's a spirit even in the things that frighten the Yankees and lead them to create the harmful stereotypes about Southerners - though admittedly, some of those stereotypes are partially warranted. There is a spirit in the woefully undereducated men tracing through the swamps and woods in their boats, filled with rifles and shotguns and mistreated hunting dogs, and in the stinky, festive atmosphere of dives and bars that are little more than shacks in sweltering tree lines.

And crowning the entire strange, muddy Otherworld of dangers and wonders is the Great Sultan of the South, King and Queen New Orleans, enthroned below Lake Pontchartrain, the "crescent city" looking out over the slave gulf. In her arms reside a good half of my dreams and at least that many of my great memories. In her is the most European of American cities, the seductive Paris of the South, with cities even for the dead and great monuments everywhere.

Nowhere else parties like New Orleans - welcome to flesh and farewell to flesh! No other city has weekend long block-parties every weekend in an entire district. To see Bourbon street and Decatur street and Frenchman's filled with the wandering drunks, old and young, ugly and pretty, to hear the music emanating from every club-door, to smell the nauseating smells emanating from narrow alleys - it's the Elysium of the depraved and the home of countless spirits who get riled up and party with the human beings. They party at funerals; they love life and they raise life-force up so high that it rains down from the sky and becomes part of the mud of the river. The savage and wild religions of Africa never vanished off anywhere; their spirit is evergreen, right here. The animism of the natives is alive. Old Europe is alive here, too.

Nowhere else drinks as much, pukes as much, feels the shrieking spirit of life as much as New Orleans. In her heights are the best of souls, in her depths the very darkest and most degraded. On her streets, the remains of the past are still alive and walking along with the present living.

And I know what it means to miss New Orleans. I understand Mr. Armstrong fully when he sings:

"Do you know what it means to miss New Orleans
And miss it each night and day?
I know I'm not wrong... this feeling's gettin' stronger
The longer I stay away.
Miss them moss covered vines...the tall sugar pines
Where mockin' birds used to sing
And I'd like to see that lazy Mississippi...hurryin' into spring.

The moonlight on the bayou......a creole tune.... that fills the air
I dream... about magnolias in bloom......and I'm wishin' I was there."

III. Darkness in the Pot, Darkness in the Cradle

Mother Swamp is the common cradle of all this life and power. And she was my cradle. In her dark bosom, I wandered as a child, only dimly aware of the immensity of it all, but more aware than other kids, I think. My people cooked dark crawfish bisque and etoufees, and made very dark gumbos that bubbled full of different lumps and shapes and ingredients - rice, crawfish, crab, chunks of vegetables - like little swamps in a pot. It was so spicy, it made you feel warm and glowing. That spice is just another manifestation of the vibrancy of my home; life-fire rises when spicy things go inside your throat and belly, because fire and those spices have a spiritual, hidden relationship.

Swamps and bayous were normal to me. So were the downsides of the sorts of people you might meet on the swamps and bayous. My father is a good man, but when he was younger - and when I was much younger - he wasn't always very careful about the sorts of people he hung around, especially these friends he had through his hunting club. I hate hunting, and always have. I think maybe I disappointed my father a bit by not eagerly joining him in hunting like all the other little sons of his friends did. But it wasn't my nature; my mother's somewhat softer touch triumphed in me on this point of developing personality.

My parents divorced when I was one year old. But my father got visitations with me every other weekend, and as I grew up, I saw him on a semi-regular basis. Often enough, after I was old enough, he'd spend weekends with me at the camp which was the home-base of his hunting club. It was on a bayou somewhere in Lafourche Parish. On the whole, I hated most of it because it meant having to be around his brutish friends. These men who styled themselves as "sportsmen" or "hunters" were all walking desecrations of the sanctity of those Spanish moss-hung woods and wetlands.

They didn't take their dogs and guns out on boats, to tromp through slues and muddy woods, with any hint of respect for the creatures they killed. My Cajun ancestors, they took respectfully. This was something else. They were mostly young, most were sheriff's deputies (but of course, anyone could be a deputy if they or their family knew the sheriff well) and they were clearly quite bored and frustrated with their lives, only feeling really strong and alive by getting tanked up, killing things, and bragging with friends. Hunting is a pervasive part of the culture of the South, and as much as my experience of it was mostly negative, I still hold out a hope that someone out there does it with a better heart.

One weekend, (I think I was about 7 or 8) my step-brother and I were waiting at the boat-landing to leave and go to the camp, and some of my dad's friends were standing around their trucks, getting dogs unloaded and onto boats to make the trip. My father was already in his boat, trolling along, and my brother and I were waiting to ride with someone else. There was a problem with one of the dogs; for whatever reason, this dog was older and no longer really able to perform as his masters needed. I recall it was a white and brown patchy dog with long hound-like ear flaps, like all of these hunting dogs.

Wilbert, a friend of my father's - and one of the older members of his pals group - dragged the dog off of the bed of a truck, and called out to another of the guys there, asking him something about what a ".410 would do", and then placed a shotgun of that gauge to the side of the dog's head and shot it. This happened quickly; it was a shock to me, but immediately painful when the dog didn't die; howling in shock and pain, it ran, badly injured, and hid under a truck. The laughing company managed to drag it out a bit, with one - Rick, I believe his name was - yelling a warning about getting the dog's blood on his truck. Another crack from the shotgun, and the dog was dead.

It happened fast, but slow, sort of a slow nightmare type-time. The dog's body was cast into the bayou right off the boat ramp. My face had crumpled into tears by this point, and I stood staring at the floating, foamy corpse of the beast, seeing its blood leaking out and making dark clouds in the water. There was blood in the bayou and it just kept spreading, getting wider and wider. I could still hear the laughing of the gathered men, but a rage and grief had welled up in me that I couldn't comprehend fully. And the oddest thing - the bayou itself (to me) seemed to be swirling angrily, like it was reacting against this wanton crime against the sanctity of life. It was never so clear to me in my life of what was wrong or right, nor of the need for the dog's killer to join his victim, and in the same manner. People may think all this is crazy, but a young boy's eyes saw it. His young heart saw it, too. It was real. Maybe it was real in that way that only bloodshed can make things real.

The ride down the bayou to the camp was all in silence on my part, and more tears. My step brother was sad too, but I don't know if this impacted him the same way. But he was upset enough to join me in a strange memorial service we spontaneously decided to do for the dog - he read Psalm 23 out loud while I placed a piece of spongy driftwood full of yellow flowers I'd picked on the bayou, and watched it float out into the brownish water.

While I was watching it, I got the idea - without even knowing how - that the bayou could do more than carry this memorial to the dog. It seemed to me that any powerful feeling I had could be carried out through its water to some greater place, maybe making those feelings even more powerful, powerful enough to make my will real beyond myself. In my anger and hate - and even to this day I consider it righteous - I came back to that bayou an hour later and sliced away at sticks, whittling them down like I wished to whittle the necks of those evil men, and I cast them into the water, so that my angry carvings would go out somehow, and strike them down.

I wanted to rage to the trees, and I did. I could never look at those hunting dogs again - nor anytime today - and not think of that day.

Later in my life, when I began to learn the conjure-art, I came across the ages-old practices of dispersing power and the setting out of ritual items, and recognized them instantly. It's a logic every Conjure Man knows - to keep something near you, bury it on your property. To destroy something, commit it to flames. To attract something into your life, bury it under your front doorstep. To get something to leave you and vanish into the deep, toss it into running water. To truly disperse something's power, discard it at a crossroads and walk away without looking back. To get a message to spirits, bury it in a graveyard. To get it to secretly work on someone, hide it in their food or drink. To toss something into still water sinks it and rots it, eventually, but disperses it well, slowly, over time. Tossing something east makes it start or get strong; to make something end or waste away, toss it to the west.

This list continues almost infinitely, but the logic is the same- what does nature, the natural forces of the surrounding, do to the object? Where does it remain? What other environmental powers are active at the time (i.e. a rising sun, a setting sun, etc.)? If you can be aware of these things, spirits can help you to make things happen.

What I had intuitively done was dispose of my anger in a body of water - a spiritual power, a non-human person which can be experienced as a bayou - thus passing to it my curse. But the bayou power has a nature and a way of acting. Had I been more informed at 8, I could have gained contact with and the aid of the spirit of that place for my curse. I could have coaxed it to use its will to aid me and join me. As it were, I don't know if Cousin Bayou did anything, or simply dispersed those thorns of rage.

For all the problems, being in those woods at the camp was direct exposure to many sides of life and death. Drunk rednecks never make anything especially illuminated feeling, but there was something else afoot. Animal parts were everywhere, there was certainly a lot of wildness, but a starkly quiet feel in the woods. The place was reserved and resentful of these haughty men with guns who trampled down plants and animals in their ignorance, and couldn't comprehend at all the sacred realities that were present and in need of recognition and respect.

The whole land reacted to them in the same way I did emotionally, and I knew it; it spoke to me on some level. Anger, or any strong emotion, focuses us in strange ways if we're aware enough to notice. Strong emotions are doors of trance. My dreams that night, in the rainy woods, were of the wooden walls of the camp building itself coming to life and rending the flesh of these men with the nails hammered everywhere inside it. The antlered skulls of trophies also came to life, impaling them. The intensity of emotion which was awoken in me by this cruel and empty "blood sacrifice" I had witnessed was ominous and transformative.

I felt protected by those woods. I still do. Many of those men came to unhappy ends - as you might imagine, there isn't much of a future for sheriff's deputies who can't do anything except drink and shoot animals, and sometimes wave guns at people. Wrecked marriages and child support checks to resentful ex-wives, deaths in hunting accidents for one of them, and (sadly) deaths in shooting accidents for some of their children, a lot of lay-offs and one prison sentence in the mix, all in a space of **20** years afterwards, finishes my story for them.

For my own reasons, I would like to point out that these men were largely not Catholic men. One or two - including my father - were from Catholic backgrounds, and oddly, I never noticed them being so cruel or stupid as the others. I am not saying that Catholics are innately better somehow, and as always, a dumb young man with a gun is a dumb young man with a gun, no matter what religious background they come from, but they did seem to be different from the low Protestant hoot-monkeys, less vicious or more mature, more comfortable with drinking (low Protestants are against drinking, as a whole) and basically doing whatever they were doing.

I take no credit for these runs of bad luck that happened to these men, nor do I think the spirit of that place really became vengeful and struck at these men, but the latter theory wouldn't surprise me. Our own wickedness - and our lack of recognition and respect for the basic sacred things in this world - become the barbs that our souls get tangled in, and sometimes, a higher cost is paid. If there's a universal justice out there, which I sometimes think there is, I've seen it working out in its quiet, mysterious way.

I know one more thing. Birds still sing out there on that bayou, and many of the same trees are still quietly drinking water out of the ground that the dog's blood fell on. The descendants of fish and snakes and turtles that swam that bayou that filled with the dog's blood are still swimming in it. Life is moving by, unstopped and unstoppable. It's still sacred and incomprehensible at the deepest level. And that dog is still living in me, and now that you've read my words, he or she (I never found out if the dog was male or female) is in you, too.

IV. Mastery of Crossroads: Knowing Who You Are

Things in nature are like currents of power, very mysterious, and experienced in a countless number of ways. But everything, no matter how substantial it seems, is a process, or an event. Even a big rock jutting out of the bank on the side of a river or bayou is not an unchanging monolith, but an event, an always changing thing. The river power that it is in constant communion with changes it slowly. The wind does, too. Sometimes a person might. Nothing's static.

This is why flexibility of mind - and the extreme mental and spiritual flexibility of the sorcerer - is not just a wise perspective that has uses; it is more essential than that. It simply reflects the way of things. To be in touch or in harmony with all things means to be fully aware of how dynamic things are, and to not get over-obsessed with being one thing or another, yourself. If you went back to the old site of the camp and the boat launch that I told you about, you'd see practically nothing there like I saw it all those years ago. Even those brutes are nearly all gone, dispersed, moved on, dead. Life remains - trees, animals, the land and water itself - but the boats are gone, the buildings changed, the "feeling" of the area would probably be different.

Things cycle upwards in growth, or downwards in diminishment. At some point, for what seems to be a while, things are in fullness, in a breathing space of completion, before starting the downward spiral. After it's waned away totally, but before it begins again to grow in some new way, it's not one thing or the other. That precious and mysterious time is when the real truth of the situation of any creature or spirit is known. That "gap" is the open gap of mystery, the roots of a thing. Waxing and waning moons are like this, as well as full ones and dark ones.

A human life is like this in youth and adulthood and aging and the condition after what we describe as "death". When the sun is dawning or setting, it's not one way or the other, not previous night nor coming day. At this time, that power fills you up and makes you not who you were the time before, nor who you're going to be in the time to come. A person can, if they are inclined, walk off with a penny or a silver dime under their tongue, and arrive at a place where two roads cross - or any road, in a pinch - and, if they arrive at dawn or at twilight, they can speak the ill deeds they've done, or the ones they're ashamed of, and then spit that coin out, walking quickly away from it.

At a crossroads, those things will be dispersed, but on a regular road, if someone were to come by and pick up that coin (so I was told) they'd inherit the impact of those bad deeds. The real point of a trick like this is the timing - a man or woman utilizing a time where things aren't anything in particular, when a person isn't what they were, nor what they're going to be in the future. Anything is possible.

When your life is waxing, chances are, you don't know who or what you really are; but you have, with all the energy of youth, a lot of great ideas, and a lot of great hopes and dreams or fears. Nearly all of those ideas, hopes, dreams, and fears eventually show themselves to be passing phases. If you can be open to the world, when you are in fullness, you might look back and look forward and come to know who and what you are. It's better to know while you're alive than to wait until you pass into the unseen reality. If you get that knowledge while you're alive, you can be a power-worker, a conjure-man or woman, a sorcerer.

Identity is such a crisis and a quest for nearly everyone. The biggest selling cults, religions, and fashion brands all have two things in common: quick and easy identity, and quick and easy answers to life's questions tied to those identities. I've known a lot of people who belong to alternative spiritual paths, a lot of people who self-identify as Pagans, witches, and what have you. The most educated and motivated of this lot are the people who spend a lot of time and energy reconstructing Pagan cultures and religions from the past, to fill the spiritual void they feel left over from the sudden and ugly transition away from wiser, older religions into the new brands we have around.

Even though the conversion from genuine Pagan religions to Christianity happened quite a long time ago in Europe, it still haunts some people, and they feel the call, the need to worship the natural powers and to honor their non-Christian ancestors.

I consider myself quite the ancestor-worshiper. Nothing could be wrong with wisely honoring the old powers of your Ancestors, whoever they were. But to take it too far, and begin ignoring who you are now, and what land is below your feet, and grasping at an identity born in a culture that has largely passed away and transformed, like many have, is counterproductive. I've known people who got lost in that.

When you encounter the unseen powers, they don't really want to hear about just your ancestors when they look into you and ask who you are. If you want to be respected by spirits, have any hint of influence with them, you have to be centered in real identity, not fantasies about what some ancestors might have been doing long ago, or invented personas that don't go as deep.

Real identity starts in the ground and the blood. Your homeland, and the land upon which you lived and experienced powerful life-transitions and experiences, is a large basis for who you are. Most people don't grasp this fully, but it's vital. Louisiana shaped the "human event" that is me; nearly everything about me that is powerful, useful, or precious is there because of where I come from. My blood, the culture of my people and the heritage passed on to me from them, also shapes me.

The entire countryside west of Interstate 10, along the River Road, with all its plantation houses, and bayous, is not just a place to me; it's also my internal landscape- the places I went around when I was a kid. Baton Rouge, Brusly, New Orleans, Lafayette, Bayou Sorrel, New Iberia, Grosse Tete, Bayou Lafourche, Lake Verret, Lake Pontchartrain, Lake Maurepas, Lake Des Allemands, Bayou Maringouin, Plaquemine, Saint Gabriel, White Castle, Napoleonville, Lutcher, La Place, Nottoway, St. Louis, Mulberry Grove, Belle Alliance, Oak Alley, Destrehan, Grammercy - they read like the names of spirit-world locations to me. They have that impact on me.

They were around me all my life and spirits and powers of these places chiseled me out of flesh. They were there when I sat in fishing boats in the Atchafalaya Basin, or on the Mississippi River with my grandfather as he hauled in nets full of catfish, bass, turtles, and crawfish. One of those turtles - affectionately called "a snapping turtle" - pierced my belly-button when I held it too close to me, once.

I remember that sting and my blood on my bare belly, falling into the mud in the boat. I remember my grandfather drinking the water straight from the river; today, I wouldn't dare, for fear of pollution, but as a child, I didn't know better, and didn't mind. But part of being one with a land is taking its waters and its animals and foods into you.

There are ancient bones in the ground in Louisiana and in the Americas- ancient burial mounds, every bit as ancient or powerful as the burial mounds in Europe, or any Stonehenge. Our rivers here are just as ancient as any that flow elsewhere.

The most powerful thing I can say to a spirit is the name my people gave me, and to tell it who those living people are- the people of South Louisiana, of Acadiana, people from Spain and France, from Belgium and England, but who came here and wed themselves to the blood of natives and became parts of this land. The most powerful thing I can do is tell the spirit what's unique about me, what I love, and lean my feet on the ground and wait for that same earth who knows me so well to speak on my behalf.

The spirit will know that I am a person of bayous and lakes, of street corners and cemeteries in New Orleans, a person of swampy forest and long stretches of interstate and highway. I don't just say it, I feel it. There's Catholic in me, some Vodou, some Native religion; there's European culture, African, and Indian. To be someone from Louisiana, on this day, in this year - it's a real, living group of people with a real living power. It means something specific, something important to the spirits. It gives you a form of self-knowledge, self-confidence, and leverage.

The Ancestors were very wise. They just lived on their land, understanding the people and culture to which they were joined, and respecting and worshiping the powers of their land and people, all in a spontaneous, easy way. I always work to be that way myself.

That's what I do when I go outside. Wherever I am, whatever land

I'm on, there are always sacred powers there - trees, woods, fields, swamps, rivers, roads, buildings, family homes, and (sometimes) oceans. To walk out next to these things or onto these things or into these things - that's spiritual communion. That's a spiritual meeting, if you can see it right, with your other eyes. As a true "dirt worshiper", I honor those things, and earth below and sky above as parents. I don't even bother with "names" really; they are what they are - Great Mother Earth, Cousin Bayou, Old Man River, Sister Willow, Brother Oak, Old Man, Great Forest, Grandmother, Grandfather, even Gran Hibou.

I'm a master of crossroads, so I claim my heritage and roots as identity, and use it to befriend, seduce, or even (rarely) to threaten spirits. But finally, I'm even more than my roots - like all beings, there's something about me that isn't this or that, and standing at the crossroads inside means having access to who you are and who you're not, the possibility of "going any which way". A two-headed, two-faced sorcerer, I celebrate what I am and what I'm not at will.

V. Ms. Ava's Feeding-Place

Most of the old people that were alive when I was growing up - most of my neighbors - spoke Cajun French as a first language, or had parents who did. I didn't hear the sounds of their extreme accents, nor hear their words like I do now; as a child it was just normal to me. I had to get out and experience a blander America - even some towns north of Alexandria, where there is no little or no Cajun or Catholic culture - before I could appreciate how exotic and unique they really were as people.

And they were (at times) wise people. They were all Catholic, of course, though some were (like myself) not terribly great Catholics, at least by the book standards. They were inheritors of some wisdoms and some ways of seeing the world which were a real asset. I wish more survived them, but not much did. If I had to pick one thing to survive, it wouldn't be any folk charm they might have known nor any piece of now-forgotten local history; it would be their happy outlook on life, and their love of food and family. Those are things that mean everything to me, too. I think I got it from them.

They were all obsessed with three and nine. Those numbers keep coming up in any Catholic society, but also in societies before the Catholic church's birth. Three is easy enough to understand, but nine is more than just three times three. Nine is the mother of things, the source that everything comes back to, because no matter what you multiply by nine, if you add all the digits of the result up, they always equal nine. Strange thing that, but a spiritual thing. And three - well, there's three of everything. There's three things about you and every person or being; there's what you don't know about yourself, what you only partially know or glimpse in feelings and dreams, and what you do know- what you look like, what you remember of your past, and the like.

That's why saying things three times is so important, or doing them three times is so important, if you want to fix them into place magically. Every situation or power or being has a mystery about it, what we can't consciously know about it, but also what's half-known or partially known, and then what's fully known. To say it or do it three times makes your act apply to all three levels of reality. Tripling that into nine times make the act three times more powerful - an exponential increase in force.

I do believe Ms. Ava, a neighbor of mine when I was growing up in Vacherie, was my first teacher about the importance of trinities. Though Catholic, she never got tired of pointing out how many ancient religions had trinities in them. In a sense, the Holy Spirit was (for her) what we do know and feel about God, and Jesus was what was only partially known- we only have vague stories and hints about his historical character, and he was tricky, always talking in double meanings - and God himself was mysterious, beyond humans, just using Jesus as a mask for meeting men and women half-way and revealing himself the best he could.

Ms. Ava also carried on spirit-feeding under the live oak outside her back door. The leftovers and leavings of every meal she cooked ended up in one particular area, and she always told me that it was good to "give back to the earth" anytime you eat. Her "feeding place" was swirling with power; local minor spiritual forces and persons had learned that this woman was worth hanging around. And she always plopped down the food-remains in three scrapes or servings.

I last saw Ms. Ava (she never got married, for some strange reason) just about two years ago - very old now, but hanging in there. I'm glad I saw her then, because I don't know if I'll ever see her in this human world again. But I am glad that she was there for my childhood.

When I lived in New Orleans, and got to learn folklore and even the lores of hoodoo and other native-influenced styles of sorcery from people and places there, I always thought of people like Ms. Ava, and realized that they had, without even realizing it, a touch of this, a taste of this, a real presence of this sort of wisdom in their own lives. They used it for different reasons, for different things, in different ways, but it was all from the same place. Conjury is like that; each man or woman takes it to a different place, does something different with it, lives it differently.

The library at my old grade school had a book, a blue book, with a white pentagram on the back cover. I don't remember what the name of the book was, but it was probably the first I ever found and read and was strangely in love with. Why it would be in a library for primary school kids, I have no idea, but I'm glad it was. It was on the shelf next to a book about the Bell Witch. By eighth grade, we had taken a field trip to the University of New Orleans, and at the bookstore, I bought a book of charms and talismans. I had also acquired a tarot deck by that time, which I had to hide under my shoe drawer from my mother.

My mother had loved astrology when she was in her teens, and on the shelves in our house library, she still had those astrology books.

On Saturday mornings, when I was up early for cartoons, I'd sneak into the library and grab those books and read them in bed. Before I had made it into High School, I had tried to make my first talismans - I didn't have parchment, but I had construction paper of the proper planetary colors, so I cut round shapes from the paper, used yarn to wear them around my neck, and drew the proper sigils onto them. Late at night, I'd open the window to my room and bathe them in moonlight to "charge" them, and I kept them hidden in the pages of books on high shelves, books I knew my parents wouldn't look at.

It wasn't until I mastered prayer and trance that I was able to access the spiritual forces that turn simple charm-playing into real sorcery. And that didn't happen until I was 22, when I met my first teacher of hoodoo and conjure. On my 27th birthday, sitting naked and half submerged in water, late at night, I was taken. Something pulled me out further into the water, and down under it, where there was an island under the water, an island full of dead people and insects and plants.

A spirit on the island, who looked sort of like a big tree greeted me. He was very old and majestic (and terrifying in his way) - and he gave me the greatest gift of all - Hibou, a spirit that appeared to me as an owl, to be my "head protector" and teacher and doer of my work. I remember what he said and did to me, changing me in the conjure-way, and then springing up from the water, leaping around and feeling as though I had really become an owl. For weeks afterwards, I felt a strange knot of some kind in my belly - the tangible presence of the spirit. It could speak to me, as clearly as any human could. To this day, I maintain a relationship with that power. That was the day, those years ago, when I became an Owl Doctor.

I've spent a good bit of time here talking about my past, and some things I wanted to say. Now I'll start to talk about my present, and things I do to make Conjury happen. But it was important for you to hear these things, to read them, so that some questions you might have later will have answers.

Part II:
Dream-Visions and Serpent-Weave

"Brother, if you want mo' preachin',
Save a little for me.
Glory Hallelujah! Drinking gin ain't against my teachin'!
Treat me with equality.
Now from dat small it is plain to see,
Dat somebody is holdin' out on me.
So, brother, if you want mo' preachin',
Save a little for me."

-Traditional

I. The Shape of Things to Come

My introduction is now over. If you've read this far, you know a lot about where I'm from and why I am the way I appear. This work, "Blood in the Bayou" is about how I conjure, not really about me. But the way I've experienced things in this strange work, I've come to the conclusion that you can't separate the conjury from the person working it. I touched on this before, but it has to be repeated- there are no identical conjure-folk. For all of our similarities as human beings, no two lives are the same. Every minute of your day is experienced, from your perspective, as though only you lived it.

When I saw the hunting dog killed by Mr. Jackass, all those years ago, I can assure you that only I, standing there, felt what I felt- rage and grief. The rude company of beings around me experienced various levels of amusement. But it was the same event, right? If you had asked one of those men out there "Hey - don't you see a sacred living creature being brutally killed on this boat ramp?" They would have said "what? no... there's just a fucking dog out there."

Get it straight, and don't forget it: how we see and feel co-creates (in tandem with incomprehensible forces that surround us) a world or reality that we have to live in, and we can scarce understand the worlds of others. A cunning man or woman has to understand this, because they can understand the worlds of others better if they know how the construction's being done, at every moment. Flexibility of mind is about understanding and accepting that "how it is" for you isn't "how it is" for others, and knowing that the shape of things right now in your world is going to be different from the shape of things to come.

The cunning mind slips free of the nets of rigidity and finds the fluid undercurrent of things. When you feel it for yourself, you can induce it, to an extent, in others. This strange mystery can be transmitted, in various ways. When a cunning mind is free enough, it exudes some strange presence - a weird presence - which bothers rigid minds. But it seeps into some like moisture, and causes some puddles and rot. A conjure man or woman has to be able to channel some change, has to have a faith in the malleability of things, has to know how insubstantial things are.

I'm a river of thinking, feeling, imagination, and expansive feelings of strangeness, like all people. The difference between me and good Mr. Jergens down the street is that I'm in my soul-boat on the river enjoying the ride, and he's busy trying to build castles of stone and steel on foundations of water. Life's too much work for people that have to know everything and know all the "rules" that they imagine must exist. Honestly, I'm kind of drifting along right now, not knowing really what's coming next.

But sometimes I do know. In the next three essays, I'm going to outline some spiritual and practical perspectives regarding conjury, mystical herbology and spirit-talking that I have found to be invaluable throughout the years. But tomorrow, I don't know; they might lose their value, for me, or for you. Maybe a week from now. Maybe never.

If they go the way of the dodo, my helping spirit, Hibou, will help me to find new methods and other flaming crap that will burn out in its own good time. What matters is, before it burns out, I'll have used it to make charms, talk to more spirits, heal myself and others, and see the shape of things to come. And then the ride will move on to the next place, with no one in the audience knowing what to expect.

Get comfortable with uncertainty, and you'll always be ready for what comes next.

II. Life Feeds on Life (or better yet, Life is the Feeding)

A dead hero of mine - a wise woman by the name of Val Plumwood - wrote a superb scholarly essay (in my opinion it was the entire reason she ever existed) entitled "Tasteless: Towards a Food-Based Approach to Death." This essay propelled me out of my skin and into the great web-work that is life, with every form flowing into every other. I'm living here now, in this flesh, but it is not my true home; my true home is inside of trees, birds, alligators, snakes, other humans, and in the ground.

I'm tense, at times. I know that I'm perched in a human shape like a toad, bundled up like an owl in a tree, waiting to leap or fly out suddenly. The power out there is calling to everyone and everything, calling at any time to yank it and change it. There is no stability except to prepare for the call at any moment, and be comfortable with that. It's not such a bad thing; we leap out into greater power.

Ms. Plumwood's essay is great - a work of great sorcery - because it shatters rigidity in the human mind, and it uses the element of food and eating to do it. Food and eating food are such basic functions and such common functions, that we seldom stop to think about what's really going on when we eat. This gets wild, but before it gets that way, let me suggest that you turn into a snake before we continue.

Snakes are things that can coil up tight, or get really straight, and wind around things, and slide down into things. They can go underground, through water, into walls, up pipes, into drink machines, into cars, into engines, into trees, under logs, and into boots and clothing. You can find them everywhere. They get around. So does the cunning mind, and so does the human spirit, very much like the non-human spirit persons out there. Being human, we have the anchor of flesh and the mirror of mind to complicate the matter, but as pure spirits, we'll just have the lightning flash and roar of unseen things and crazy mental winds to blitz us around.

It's not a surprise that snakes and sorcerers have been so associated, nor is it a surprise that snakes and creator spirits are associated, and magical spirits. The snake is a sorcerer among animals, hissing a powerful song that causes trances nearly everyday. I need to be a snake to show you something, and I need you to be a snake to listen. Get flexible! Uncoil in mental space and writhe along now.

I've eaten cream of wheat tonight. I like to boil up that stuff with some brown sugar or honey, or sometimes salt, pepper, and butter. It's good either way. I ate it, and down my central body hole it went. It got to my caves and tubes, and met up with some other powers that live in me - corrosive, horrid powers. They split the skulls of those little wheat bits into a million pieces and stole their power, and began carrying them off. The hard parts that the corrosive powers couldn't make heads or tails of, they banished to lower, swampy and dark chambers, where watery horrors will eventually eject these remnants from my body (and hopefully) into a cool body of water. From that body of water, they'll go deep into the earth and into other tanks and dark places.

As for the other stolen power - the kind that wasn't turned to shit - it will be carried about, and fed to great and hidden furnaces all over my being, used by living powers that carry my very life and consciousness to create the life-force. In flashes of fire they are consumed and a spark of life released.

It's mixing into me, making me who I am, this moment. I live, and that life isn't separate from the wheat itself. Brother wheat - before it was ground down and packed into a box of Cream of Wheat mix, it was hidden deep down in the earth, dragging the warmth of the sun from the surface into itself, along with waters in the dirt. Miraculous transformations happened; the seed broke and tendrils ran out, and they found the sun. A pulsing tower of green life force, it rose higher, taking wind and sun and soil-force into itself, a non-human person's house and personal feast of energy.

It turned more rigid and blonde, and was cut down by the cutting power of some harsh steel. It was lifted by human hands, blown, cut further, stacked, packed, sold, moved by the will of many beings, across many lands, collecting so many strands of power. It was processed, and it came into my hands, and was consumed.

The effort of other humans, the heat of hissing serpent-filled water and flame, the sun, the wind, water from rain and the sky and the ocean, the mingling of other plants (like sugar cane) the manure and waste of animals in the fertile ground feeding the roots of the wheat- snake along with me through the mandala of countless powers that were all packed into that spoon of cream of wheat before it went into my mouth, to be subjected to the collection of countless powers that is called (temporarily) "me."

Snake through the cracks, my friends - when you see all of the powers collected into the mosaic of life, you can see through them. Don't hang on to reason in this matter; just go through the cracks like a snake. Eating is a point where we consume power, and countless lives and other powers, and make them part of us, before they move on beyond us, and we into others. I say "eating" but consumption is a better word. All of the parts of this kaleidoscope of powers are consuming something.

Everything eats, even spirits. What they eat may be different, but the process of consuming and transforming through merging with something and changing it is constant. And it is a process, a reality, that joins us with everything else. No one is exempt! No matter how exceptional humans think they are, they are part of the shit list, part of the dinner menu, part of the buffet of powers living alongside others.

In Ms. Plumwood's essay, she writes:

"Two encounters with death led to my becoming radically dissatisfied with the usual western selection of death narratives -- both Christian-monotheist AND modernist-atheist. I think both major traditions inherit the human exceptionalism and hyper-separation that propels the environmental crisis. However, there are encouraging signs of a developing animist consciousness and mortuary practice that challenges exceptionalism and grasps human of death in terms of reciprocity in the earth community.

Some years ago, as an already established environmental philosopher, I had a close encounter with food/death, death as food for a large predator. I was seized by a Saltwater Crocodile, largest of the living saurians, heirs to the gastronomic tastes of the ancient dinosaurs. By a fortunate conjunction of circumstances I survived - slightly tenderized, but basically set aside for another occasion. Since then it has seemed to me that our worldview denies the most basic feature of animal existence on planet earth - that we are food and that through death we nourish others.

The food/death perspective, so familiar to our ancestors, is something the human exceptionalism of western modernity has structured out of serious comment. Attention to human foodiness is tasteless. Of course we are all routinely nibbled both during and after life by all sorts of very small creatures, but in the microscopic context our essential foodiness is much easier to ignore than in one where we are munched by a noticeably large predator.

Modernist liberal individualism teaches us that we own our lives and bodies, politically as an enterprise we are running, experientially as a drama we are variously narrating, writing, and/or reading.

As hyper-individuals, we owe nothing to nobody, not to our mothers, let alone to any nebulous earth community. Exceptionalised as both species and individuals, we humans cannot be positioned in the food chain in the same way as other animals. Predation on humans is monstrous, exceptionalised and subject to extreme retaliation.

Horror movies, stories and jokes reflect our deep-seated dread of becoming food for other forms of life: horror is the wormy corpse, vampires sucking blood and sci-fi monsters trying to eat humans ("Alien 1 and 2"). Horror and outrage greet stories of other species eating live or dead humans, various levels of hysteria our nibbling by leeches, sandflies, mosquitoes and worms. Dominant concepts of human identity position humans outside and above the food chain, not as part of the feast in a chain of reciprocity. Animals can be our food, but we can never be their food. Human Exceptionalism positions us as the eaters of others who are never themselves eaten."

* * *

Life is a big snake, coiling into knots that become what we see as individual beings and entities, and then coiling and slithering back through those knots. Not for no reason did the old Vodouisants say that a great snake Lwa - Damballah - created the world by slithering across the landscape and leaving valleys and pushing up mountains! Life itself is serpentine. Life eats life. Life transforms life. Ms. Plumwood knows this better than anyone; she died from a snakebite a few years after she wrote the essay from which you just read an excerpt.

If your mind gets flexible enough, it becomes serpentine. If you make a hissing noise with the wind from a full breath, forced slowly and steadily through your teeth, so that it even whistles a bit, and do it over and over while relaxing the body, eventually a majestic trance arises, and dreams can be summoned, as the serpent in you is stirred by the sound.

That "hyper-individual" that we are taught to believe in is a dime store joke. This is not to say we should just let ourselves die (I'll just be a fake hyper-individual for a little while longer, thank you very much) but something about us has to die - our ideas that we are so very wonderful and special and different from everything else, exempted from the realities that bind all things. To quote Mr. Palahniuk: "You are not a beautiful and unique snowflake. You are the same decaying organic matter as everyone else, and we are all part of the same compost pile."

Is this sounding grim? Maybe you think you've heard it all before. Maybe you have. You aren't supposed to be having an opinion right now; I asked you to become a snake a few paragraphs back (I think). Snakes just slither around. So do me and yourself a favor - stop being so cerebral and start being more reptilian. Go down to that serpent brain, deep under the human brain. There's power down there, if you keep going down through the rot and away from the ideas and lies and lies. A sorcerer isn't a hyper-individual. They are a serpent-person, a meta-entity. Go in the other direction - give up and go down further, and you'll burst from the other side, and find something you didn't expect.

What do you think lies at the bottom of the snake-pit, at the bottom of the serpentine DNA strands that make up everything alive and in the flesh? Not a magic lamp that spits out life, or a Jehova God; it's a collective of powers that are a totality, the totality. Most people expect something else. It's an odd place, a mind-blowing place, but if you leave your mind at the door, and go as a snake, you can make some good time and get something good out of it. You'll feel that damn snake the next time the life force tickles at the bottom of your spine, when a sufficiently attractive man or woman comes your way. The snake wants to come up then, flow up and into them, and take them into you, and mingle and spit out a new kaleidoscope of life.

The process is exhilarating. Life is exhilarating. You are the exhilaration, not a boring person with a job and a collection of occult books and a computer. I mean, you might be partly a boring person with a mortgage and a job and a boss you can't stand, but it would be better if you were an exhilarated force of weirdness and shape-shifting power.

Okay, I'm just racking around now - it wouldn't be better if you were that; you don't have any choice but to be that, because that's what everything is - a power flowing about and vibrating with life's joy. You don't have a choice or a preference in the matter. How much you aren't aware of this, how much you've let dull forces condition you far from this awareness, is the measure of just how far you are from the truth, and just how shocked you're going to be when the death-snake comes to bite you and restore you to the truth about things.

Give up on what you think you have, and accept some new possibilities. Go flowing, snake-boy, snake-girl, whoever you are. You'll find that the rest of the world is already doing it. Things connect to each other, and until you learn to see the serpent-weave, the tails and heads all touching, you won't get hoodoo or conjury. Why do you think this plant or that coin or that root or that color or that bone is associated with this or that charm? Because in the serpent-net of reality, they touch, they are one. They look quite different, seem far apart, but we're all coiled up in the power of it all. Catch the snake's wholeness, and you can do sorcery, because the powers can fill you and make it work.

This is how the sorcerer sees. This drunken stupor is full of fire and the light of understanding, unlike the prison for drunks that the rest of the world lives in. And quite suddenly, it changes.

II. Suddenly, It Changes: Snake-skin, Change-skin

I love crawfish. I can eat countless pounds of them in many prepared forms, any chance I get. I won't eat them raw, but might if I was desperate. Once, my dad found a dead guy in the bayou near his camp. This guy had fallen out of his boat, and been actually hit by his own outboard motor-blade, and knocked unconscious, and drowned. My dad found him floating, and dragged him into his own boat, and

brought him out, and waited until the police arrived. My dad even knew the guy - everyone knows everyone out there.
My dad told me a special detail which, back then, bothered me a bit. When he found the dead body, it was covered with crawfish, eating it. Now THAT is an image I have in my head just about every time I sit down to a fresh, crimson red steaming pile of those bugs. Am I eating some of that guy? In a way, yes. I'm certainly eating crawfish, and they ate countless powers. I'm having holy communion with all of nature. Every day, every time I eat.

Yes, I'll even eat dead people, and so will you. And one day, something's going to eat you. If you come down and die in the Atchafalaya, I might get to directly eat some of you when I buy crawfish one day in the future. I don't want to eat any of you in particular, but the idea of doing so really isn't so shocking. Life power consuming life power is the way of things. Some of my vegetarian friends can't handle this idea.

I say some because some of them only do the vegetarian thing for reasons of personal health. Others have their own brand of "big brown eye syndrome", which I assure you can be cured by seeing the big brown eyes of a lion bearing down on them as they try to run away across the savanna. Persist in denial and die confused! Vegetarians that hate people for eating crawfish need to understand that crawfish eat us, too. It's fair. It's the way of things.

Our disgusting factory farms that torment animals and keep them packed together in painful, unhealthy ways, are abominations. I agree with the vegetarians on this point, and strongly suggest that everyone who is interested in being a spirit-worker try their best to get meat and animal products from sources that are local, organic, and not factory farmed, to the best of their ability. Just don't get carried away; shit happens to animals and to humans alike. A good heart is a good heart, regardless.

When you put yourself in the serpent of consuming, celebrating force, nothing really scares you or disgusts you anymore. Everything becomes a party, in a way. I become even more kin to spirits and powers. They don't hate me so much anymore, and I don't hate myself so much anymore. Would you really hate your own left hand? Your own right eye? I hope not. The power of the totality can't hate you for the same reason. We all have our place, and our flow through many places. This is the basis for respecting all forms of life- they are part of our real body, which extends far beyond this flesh.

I hope you're still a snake, because we aren't done. Not even a weird tangent about crawfish eating dead bodies should be taken as a sign that I want you changing back into your human shape. Not yet. Look at me - scolding you about not hissing and crawling on your belly while I'm typing away over here! Well, I'm a Docteur of conjure, so I can transform into a snake that has arms and hands, and still has enough presence of mind to type. So, all is well.

IV. Dream a Little Dream of the Serpent Weave

So everything flows into everything else. You can use your eyes to find the flow and the weave and perceive it. Use color to start it - and don't bother getting hung up on "material things" - even ideas and concepts fall into the weave of life. Take gold. Gold, the metal, was wealth. Wealth got people all the comforts of life; it was stability and security, of a type. Gold is a color, too; sunlight is golden. Wheat is golden. Wheat - food - wealth - survival - security - gold - golden color - sunlight - they all run together, a family of power, close to one another in the weave. Warmth is in there, too. Fire can be golden. Fire...warmth...gold...light...it all has a strange relationship.

Snakes are long and phallic. Phalluses seek purchase to spew the liquid of generation, and thus, since time out of mind, both phallic shapes and serpents have been seen as symbols of fertility and life. Bulls and horses have large penises. Snakes emerge from dens and holes in the ground; the enormous penises of these animals, like most penises, gradually "snake out" and emerge and get longer and longer, not unlike a snake coming out. Ancient people's minds saw these things and saw connections that we don't. Bulls were the common sacrifice to Gods of fertility in the old days; bulls are still honored for great virility. But herds of cows and horses were also wealth to those who had them. Security, stability, and power. Life-power in a dozen different, related forms.

Dark mud in the swamp is black. Night is black, darkness, darkness underground, earth, the grave, nighttime, unconsciousness, many associations with the planet Saturn. But earth is also fertile, giving plants, homes to snakes, emerging life, hidden potential. Red is the color of fresh blood - shed in violence, but also in menstrual flow, which is a sign of fertile potential. When people are hurt, they bleed and get red. When they are angry, they flush red and warm. Anger, violence, fertility, life power; blood, heat, warmth, intense emotion...these things are all facets of a common reality, a common serpent-weave. And you can start anywhere in nature or in your life and build associations like this. You can begin to walk the weave with your mind and find families of power.

When a root looks like a hand, you can be sure that this power is showing you something about its nature, and how connected to human hands it really is. When a root looks like a little knobby man, or a penis, or a pregnant woman, you can see a connection, as plain as day. A little silver coin is shiny and round like the full moon. Glinting, reflecting light like the moon, silvery like the moon's light, roundness like the moon - they are connected, no matter how different or separate they may otherwise appear.

Life is a kaleidoscope of powers, and death is a name we give to the constant shifting of the lens.

V. Dream a Little Dream of Spirits

Dreams are another aspect of living power, another set of powers

gran bois

within the massive weave of things. Only idiots ignore dreams or think that they are just background noise in the head during sleep. They are more than that; they are the mind's inexhaustible vibrancy, transmitting within the strange power that is the subtle, omnipresent medium of the mystery of life. On the ocean of dreams, spirits can come to you and give gifts or messages. On that same ocean, predatory powers can assault you and even harm you.

To learn to understand dreams, one just has to understand life's strange inter-connected nature, and how insubstantial and transformative it all is. Once you are comfortably knowledgeable with respect to the truth of what you call your "outer life", you'll get the hang of the inner life. They are, after all, one life. Dream interpretation is an important part of the craft of the sorcerer from every age. Dream-visions are the most common way that spirits can really and truly reveal things to us and talk to us, because when we relax into sleep - a real "letting go" - we make ourselves open to things about the world and ourselves that we spend our waking hours ignoring.

Once, I wanted to get the ear and aid of spirits to help. I had heard that the Lwa named Gran Bois - the Great Woods or forest spirit - was a kindly fellow, good to ask for help. I had always known about Gran Bois, since my time living in New Orleans, but I hadn't really studied up on him. I just felt like I should talk to him for no reason whatsoever. The circumstances around my decision to talk to Gran

Bois are irrelevant; it is enough to say "pay attention to whatever little circumstances, moods, feelings, or intuitions you get anytime you are preparing to contact spirits!" The powers that be can speak in that way to you, as well.

In fact, as I shall discuss in the next essay to follow this one, the very best and most powerful work comes when you stop consciously really making decisions, and just let yourself spontaneously work and do things. I call that "invisible working", and it is key to the greatest operations of power.

Gran Bois has a sign, a symbol, used to represent him during rituals or ceremonies. This science of sign and symbol is one of the most powerful ones you will ever find in your time as a conjure-man or woman; and even though there are many traditional symbols and signs for some spirits, the symbols and signs that spirits teach you are always the best for your own work. In this case, for this spirit-talking, I used the traditional "veve" of Gran Bois, a crude yet powerful drawing of a man that looks like he is part tree and leaf.

Before we continue, and for now, I need you to turn into a tree for me. A tree reaches up to the sky and deep down into the earth- another unifying power, like a snake, but different.

This sort of work, giving offerings to spirits, is done outdoors. Find a tree, which will be the pole that connects the deep worlds and the higher worlds, and your words can echo up and down it, reaching spirits. Now, when you were a snake, you didn't have to worry about yelling up and down tree-trunks; you were woven into everything.

Here's a secret - even when you're a tree, or just a human standing in front of one, you're still a snake. The weave doesn't stop just because you take on another form. So, while I say "your words can echo up and down", that's just poetry. Your words, and the power behind them, echo instantly in all places in the weave, no matter where you are, or what shape you are wearing. They just flow outwards everywhere. Spirits have long and profound hearing; they can catch most things. And they especially catch things when you start collecting items and signs and symbols that are in their family of power - for yes, even spirits are in the weave "nearer" to certain aspects of it. That's the key.

Spirits love rum almost as much as I do. Gran Bois loves green leaves, and so I got him rum and sprigs of green leaves. I drew his sign on the ground at the foot of a tree in flour. All good signs for spirits - which are just representations of those spirits - need to be simple enough to be drawn with flour or some powder. My rattle, hung with its Owl feather, was used to catch the attention of the Hibou, the owl, and both the owl and the rattle-chitter were used to catch the attention of Gran Bois. When you assemble the powers, the work becomes powerful, and you can feel it. The colors, gifts, signs, powers, locations, sounds, intentions- they come together. It is majestic!

And come together they did for me. I asked the Old One to open the doorways between this world and the next for me, the Sorcerous Old One, the true Master of Crossroads among spirits - and then, the owl and I moved on to Gran Bois. Gran Bois took his rum drink, for I poured it onto his drawn symbol. It absorbed into it; it went into him. I placed the leaves around his hands. The sound of the rattle is an invisible fire; that can be offered to him too. The tree-trunk in me, my spine, the rattle sound shakes up and down that and wakes my body up, and excites my spirit. I told Gran Bois with great respect what I needed. I asked for a dream of guidance, as well as the other things I asked for - which mainly involved safety for my long journey. And that night, I had a dream. A dream from him.

In my dream, which was both vivid and had in such a way that I realized it was from "him", I was inside my home, which had a door similar to the one I have now, but it was taller, and the window on the door was much higher than my head, so I had to stand on a table next to the door to see outside. I did, and outside, it was night. A black man came walking down my front walkway, and came up to my door. He didn't know that I was watching, as the window is designed to be one-way. I expected him to knock, but instead, he began picking the lock.

I yelled at him to get lost, but he wasn't frightened away. I jumped down and grabbed the lock from the inside, to stop him from opening it, but he opened it anyway. I was afraid; I forced the lock back closed and kept yelling. He tried to force it open again from the outside, and I resisted, causing a tug-o-war between us. I began shouting for my wife to call the police.

I woke up right around then. To be clear, I was a little confused about the dream. What could it mean? I found myself settling on two possibilities. Either he was warning me about a threat to my wife and children, or he was trying to break into my life and mind somehow, to come into me and do something. I wasn't so against that second option, because let's face it - in the serpent-weave of things, he's already in my life and mind, and I in his. But the first option was a bit daunting.

So, I asked a Vodou Mambo for a dream interpretation. I knew of her, trusted her, and didn't think it could hurt. One of her friends, also a servant of Lwa, responded to me. Her answer sets a wonderful tone, I think, for all people who wish to do dream interpretation. It made me grow in my ability, that's for sure.

Here's what she told me:

***

"My experience with dreams is that they are very personal, although there is a vocabulary of symbolism that is fairly universal. I find it best to sit with a dream, and see what comes to you over time. Usually the meaning will become apparent, especially with such a vivid dream. Houses, in the dreamscape, usually represent your mind (not your literal home). In my opinion, this dream doesn't sound like a warning. It sounds like you made a powerful offering to Gran Bwa, and that maybe the Lwa were communicating with you about the nature of the barrier between you and communication with Spirit. The lock sounds like a symbol of control, perhaps trying to control your communication with Spirit instead of letting it flow naturally. It sounds like the Lwa are trying to come into your life, and I have found them very open to communication. The hardest part for me is learning to listen!"

* * *

And as it turns out, she was absolutely right. At this chaotic time in my life, I had "let myself go", at least, as far as a sorcerer can. I had started slipping into rigidity and illusions of control. She used the key word - flow. And better yet, flow naturally. Stop being such a knob! I was a knob. But I am a knob no longer! Except on occasions when it suits me to be a knob. This fine and wise woman shocked me back. We all have to get shocked from time to time, and we have to shock others from time to time.

I have been visited by spirits in dreams many times. As my spiritual power and insight increased, their messages became more dear to me and more useful. I owe a great debt of gratitude to the unseen world. Most recently, I was finding myself more and more trapped in my house, and I began to feel very introspective, which then turned into an odd craziness. Now, no one can really tell when I'm feeling or acting crazy because I already feel and act pretty odd around most people. But this was different - it was cabin fever of a type.

In requests to the spirit-world for guidance, my typical requests, I was given a dream from a spirit that took the form of a turtle. It appeared to me as a turtle first, and then got out of its shell! To see a turtle without its shell was a bizarre thing, to say the least. It walked around, the strangest, greenest, skinniest thing I had ever seen, but with a big fat turtle head. It's wise, calm eyes never left me.

And as it turned out, he was right - getting out of my shell (again, a symbol of my house) was exactly what I needed to do. Many long walks and drives down the River Road and walks in the woods and on the river-banks later, I was feeling renewed. When spirits appear shaped like animals in your dreams or visions, use that - it's like them giving you their phone number. Visualizing that animal and locking onto it with words and sounds and messages gets what you're trying to say back to them. The turtle-person was thanked, for certain. And don't ever forget to say thank you. Being polite is as important as learning to listen.

VI. Illuminations and Representations

An "illumination" is what the Vodouisants call a dream given by a spirit, at your request, or just out of the blue. You know these dreams because they are a bit more vivid and memorable than other dreams. They come marked "priority", in other words. The best way to get them is just like I got mine from Gran Bois - ask. Make the powers all come together, and make the gifts, and ask. It doesn't have to be all formal and crazy; just bring the powers together, one night, relaxing, in your home even, over a personal shrine, and do what you do to get in "touch", and ask. Leave your offerings respectfully.

To be more formal, people use seven-day candles and put them in a white bowl of water in their bedrooms. White candles are for general purposes (like advice or guidance) and can be used for any spirit, but some say that you should get candles that are color-related in power to the spirit in question, or the one you want an illumination from. Into that water, you can toss offerings and symbols, things, or signs of the spirit. In Vodou, they wrap their washed heads in clean white cloths and sleep with them on, because they believe that evil powers can't get into your dreams if you do that, or at least, harmful powers have a harder time. As you relax to sleep, with the candle in the room lit, you have to open yourself to that spirit and drift off thinking about him or her (or it.)

Any dream that comes in the night can be your "answer" or illumination, so it's important to write them down as soon as you can, for the subtle nature of the dream-medium is such that they fade quickly for most people upon waking. The more powerful you become, the more subtle your mind becomes, the easier it will be to see and retain dreams. And again - always say thanks and give back. Spirits eat the essence of offerings, and will hang around more if you're generous.

Making representations of spiritual powers is important to me, and to all people who want to master the spirit-art. The Veve of Gran Bois is just one example; the ones you make for yourself, based on dreams or visions or just what you experience of a power in your waking life, are the best. Hibou - Old Owl - is my helping spirit, the Spirit of my Head, as it were. I have a simple symbol of him, a simple and primitive figure of an owl flanked by two simple trees, that I draw on things, including in flour or cornmeal on the ground. I drew mine just from looking at an owl in so-called "real life". How an animal is shaped to our senses is not just a fact of sense-experience, but a symbol, the power showing itself to us in a way that we can tap into it.

In my next essay, I'm going to talk about more symbols, symbols and signs of power that can be created and used, but this category that I now speak of is a different variety - these are the "signatures" of spirits, or mug-shots or portraits of them or of objects associated with them, or both. Through these things, our minds immediately home in on the family of power associated with the spirit.

When you create and look at these things, standing out from the dark ground or floor in the starkness of white, your mind merges with it, and the spirit knows. When you draw these things on walls or objects, that spiritual power is connected to it, so long as that drawing or carving stays there. This sort of "shamanic art" is as old as the hills, and still powerful, because it works on the Serpent's back - the constant mother and sustainer of all things, containing all things.

VII. The Two Owls

Once, a client came to me needing dream interpretation. I get a lot of clients who want this. This is what she told me:

"I was walking in the woods, very tall trees, mostly dirt ground and roots, and a faint sunlight coming through the top of branches. Then, kind of suddenly, two snow owls walk/waddle up to me and stand about two feet in front of me and just stare into my eyes. I remember the owls vividly: the brightest white color, with flecks of grey and brown on the feathers. One owl was bigger in size than the other, and I thought of them as a couple. Anyway, that was the dream, and I think I remember asking them, "what do you want with me?" I know I can tell you this stuff and you won't think it strange. And I couldn't help but wonder what would be the significance of this dream, if any. Something has been going on in my life lately that I am questioning."

***

My first thought upon reading this was "thank the sacred powers for this girl's spunk - asking powers what they want with you or what they have come to show you is only one of the best things you can do, if you can gather your wit enough to do it."

And I mean that. Always ask if you can.

Anyway, here was my response:

"When it comes to any sort of omen or augury, a movement of a natural force or power (like forces or powers shaped like owls) is only intelligible within a given context. Only you can know the true context of your own dream-visions. By themselves, they are just owls; likely a mated pair.

But within a meaningful context, and given the events and forces surrounding your viewing of the owls, they can take on entire realms of significance. For instance, if I did nothing tonight but drank a few more Red Stripes and hit the sack, and I dreamed of a black cat getting hit crossing the road, that would be that. An annoyingly disturbing dream, but bland to me, essentially.

However, had a client asked me to ask Hibou how their upcoming long road drive was gonna go, and I made the proper preparations, and dreamed that night the very same dream - the cat getting hit - I'd be disturbed for another reason, and suggest they alter the time of the trip. The context and events surrounding the dream/vision govern much of its significance.

I visualize you walking alone under snowy boughs and crunching across ice in the dim light and wondering if you should...remain associated with a group of people you've been associated with. You are alone, and suddenly, two snow owls fly by, struggling to remain together in the wind. The sign is clear, or at least, it is to me; at this point, you should consider staying close with these people. Had you not been wondering that, it would just be two birds.

The situation becomes a ritual. Had you lit a candle before you left and poured out a small measure of liquor or rum for the spirit that guides and protects you, asking from the bottom of your heart for it to walk with you and show you a sign, and then taken that walk, and then saw the owls while wondering, with a fixed mind, on that quandary, the owls would rise to the level of full-blown omen, a full-blown answer.

Are owls meaningful to you in some deeper way? I know they are to me. Snow owls are white. Two symbols build: the owl, and whiteness. Dead bodies become white and bloodless. snow and ice are white. Rigid and hard, clear and crystalline, freezing without warmth. Purification through freeze and ice. Purification through death. Sudden halt in motion and warmth and movement. Quiet. There are the associations born of white. Cleanness, but also halt and death and freeze. Purification. Clarity in silence. It's never more quiet than when the earth and trees are blanketed in snow at night, and ice crystals whisper along in the air.

Owls are already night birds, and they can move through darkness and obscurity easily due to their great hearing - not sight, as most people think. They can guide themselves through the darkest of places with ease, and they fly silently, as they alone have a natural flight-noise dampening system on their wing feathers. Where they go, they go in silence and stealth, usually surprising those prey they strike, when they strike. Like death, which slips along quietly and unexpected, and strikes suddenly.

Because they are at home in the dark, and can move about so easy in it, Owls are associated with finding lost things. And, of course, occult wisdom and mysticism and sorcery. Very much like the stuff I've told you here."

* * *

She went on to tell me the specific situation she was concerned about, and her dream then made perfect sense.

VIII. Went on Down to the Crossroads

I just realize that I forgot to ask you to stop being a tree. If you are a good reader, you're still a tree right now, just the sort that can read. Now, become a snake again. Be all things again. Be a person and a snake. Each person is standing at a crossroads, and in fact, each person is a crossroads. In us, many powers from every direction meet, come together.

Many different cultures, religions, families (seen and unseen) races of man, times of man, places of man, all meet in us, and everyone is like that. You become a serpent-person, a two-headed entity, a Master of Crossroads, when you believe that, know it, and feel it.

Part III:
Spirit-Talking, the Invisible Work and the Great Darkness

"I went to the crossroad
Fell down on my knees;
I went to the crossroad
Fell down on my knees...
Asked the Lord above "Have mercy, now;
Save poor Bob, if you please."
Standin' at the crossroad
I tried to flag a ride;
Standin' at the crossroad
I tried to flag a ride...
Didn't nobody seem to know me
Everybody pass me by.
The sun goin' down, boy,
Dark gon' catch me here."

-Robert Johnson

I. The Hollow Bone and The Secret Village

The first two parts of this work on conjury were theoretical, mostly. This part and the final portion will be practical - they will be collections of sorcerous lore and practical criteria for contacting and manipulating something extraordinary. Of course, in the system of life, the serpent-entwined swamp of reality, writhing and changing in its sacred pulse, there is no such thing as a one-way ride. When I say this, I mean that all actions and flows of power are recursive - an action or a flow of power may seem to change something or affect something, but it is also itself changed.

Recursion with respect to conjury is simple: Conjury does you as much as you do conjury. At the same time you're apparently changing things through laying tricks, packing mojo bags, and talking to spirits, you're being changed, too. Some don't see this, some won't see it; but the profession of the conjure man or woman, the real sorcerer, is transformative on every level. Once you're involved, you aren't the same ever again. Nietzsche famously said "when you gaze into an abyss, the abyss gazes also into you."

The transforming power of real conjury is deeply rooted in all places, because it takes its power from the most essential sacred force that underlies and animates reality. The fact that you can't get involved without being so radically changed leads to a lot of folklore about losing one's soul, mind, or sanity to the weird powers. But the reality is both more tame and more astounding than any folklore. The sorcerer's mind comes to be of practically alien character compared to others.

Those who want to work to channel the power that can change the world have to become a staging ground for that power; you have to be an inviting horse for the rider, and your mind has to become a safe environment in which strange forces can enter in and persist. A rigid mind in denial about the constant transformative power of reality, or ignorant of it, is not a territory that spiritual forces can enter in and pass through. The less you settle on "knowledge" about the outside world or yourself, and the more you let the world be as weird and unpredictable as it truly is, the stronger a channel you'll be. You'll be what they call a "hollow bone", a channel that doesn't obstruct spiritual force.

You'll also be better equipped, mentally, to deal with this world and all its savagery and uncertainty. There is a double blessing here. The less you "know", the more you gain, in a sense. The less you try to build up, the stronger and more stable you become; an old saying states "you can't fall off the floor." This isn't to suggest that a informational base about things like arts or sciences or even the occult arts can't be built up and tapped for use; but this is to say that you shouldn't let the lore you collect restrict you or convince you that it can't be any other way.

I was talking to another Conjure man the other day about recipes for hoodoo oils and powders and the like. I will expand on this topic more in my final essay, but for now, it's enough to know that a real sorcerer of the folk tradition of real southern sorcery will find time to look to the historical fund of information we have regarding old charms and potions and recipes, for use in their own work. But that alone can't be enough- when you find yourself in possession of a good recipe for something like a dust or an oil, you'll also find yourself feeling a lot of intuitions about it.

If you ignore those, you'll fall flat, at least half the time. Recipes and charms and formulae are not rigid because the serpent that spit them out, so long ago, is not rigid. If you feel the need to add something to a powder, don't ignore that feeling. It may be that the powder or dust won't "work" for you unless you do as you felt to do.

This also touches on a topic which I'll discuss soon, the topic of the "Invisible Work" - the intuitive work that emerges from the mind and soul of a conjure man or woman that really gains a connection to the source of all occult wisdom and power, that secret source that snakes through the mind and the world, forever. Intuition is an emergent property of the mind as it becomes involved in phenomenon, and some sorcerous works - the most powerful ones - are also "emergent events"- they emerge from an unknown place in you and come to life all without being planned or thought out.

Some of the powers that pass through the hollow bone of the Conjure Man or Woman are spirits. Spirits are, as I have said before, non-human persons that exist, just like we human persons exist. They have their own ecology, just as we humans do; they co-exist with other persons (human and non-human) and they co-exist with their own environment. The spirit-world or world of the invisibles is certainly an jungle of forces, just as the world you see around you right now is. Also, the invisible and the visible have a special overlap, so our ecological situation can also affect the spirit world, and vice-versa.

The whole world of unseen non-human persons is called by me "the secret village", because like humans and animals in our world, the vast population of non-human spirit persons together create much abundance, more life, and more evolutionary force.

Like the simple recursions and complex relationships that we see between living beings in our world, the unseen has its own. And again, never forget - there is a crossing-place between the two halves of reality (the objective metaphysical "crossroads") where the two halves meet and spill their influence into one another. They are together a wholeness, but they are experienced differently by human beings, as though they were separate. "Grace" refers to the experience of the totality of things that exist and appear to exist, the harmonious and dynamic fullness of things.

I have often said that every human being is a crossroads, and I mean it; this statement has many levels of meaning, but this is the highest meaning: each human mind can be a doorway to an unseen world, through which the influences and persons of that place can interact with this one and affect this one. There is a single danger - though a perilous one - with this fact of our minds and beings: if the mind is too rigid, rigid with fear or fantasies about the way things "have to be", that mind might be shaken into madness by the passage of spirits or other powers.

The flexibility I've always preached is about protecting the mind from this simple fact. The real experience of spiritual powers will be stranger than you think but also stranger than you can think. If you give up on expecting things to be a certain way, and give up on trying to explain it all, you'll be fine - should you find yourself in these extraordinary situations.

II. Thirteen Spirit-Marks

Even though there is much about spirits that we can't comprehend or know (just as there is much about ourselves we can't comprehend or know) spirits, or non-human persons of the unseen reality - in my experience and in accordance with what folklore and myths tell us - evidence the following characteristics on a fairly regular basis:

1. They have a sense of personhood, intentionality and goals, and the more powerful the spirit, the more inscrutable its motives or goals may be.

2. They occupy a complex web of relationships with other powers, beings and persons, seen and unseen.

3. They change over time, or in response to stimuli, relationships, or situations. Although they may not experience emotion as humans do, they appear to be attracted to certain things, beings, or situations, or desirous of them.

4. They can appear in many different ways to human minds that perceive them, and the more powerful the spirit, the more shapes it can take, up to and including very abstract forms.

5. They are, with few exceptions, not chained by the typical human thinking about morality; they are unpredictable at times and occupy a space of moral ambiguity.

6. Some respond well to respect and offerings of gifts, and attempt to reciprocate gifts well-given. Some spirits enter into, and maintain, relationships with human beings and are very protective of those humans or groups of humans.

7. Some (a few) are harmful to human beings and the animals or other life-forms of our world in nearly every way, and are not desirable for communication or for partnerships of any kind. Beyond this harmful type of spirit, there is no such thing as a true "good guy" or

"bad guy" spirit - spirits are a strange blend of helpful and harmful, of what humans call "good" or "evil". They defy final human judgment.

8. Most spirits are connected to certain places, or certain other phenomenon like certain sounds, symbols, natural forces, societies, animals, people, or events.

9. Spirits have various levels of force, intelligence, and will available to them to see that their own goals, intentions, or activities come to fruition- just like human beings. When two spirits come into conflict with one another, the stronger one overpowers the weaker and "gets its way", as it were.

10. Though they can seem to be eternal, most spirits change over time, and after a very long period of time, (even thousands or millions of human years) can seem to cease to be the spiritual being they once were, and never been seen or found again. Others seem to be truly immortal, able on some level to maintain some mysterious identity over countless cycles of change.

11. Some spirits (though not all) seem to have been human beings or animals in our world before, often quite a long time ago. Others have "been" other kinds of beings before, in other places, times, or worlds.

12. Many spirits are interested in human beings, and seek to join with human beings in special ways so that they can (perhaps) experience life through a human's mind and from a human's perspective. Some are also eager to be closer to humans who make efforts to contact the unseen world and make offerings to it.

13. Most spirits can perceive what a human being's emotional state is, and what thoughts or feelings are occupying their conscious mind in the present. Some are "clairvoyant" and can know things about the past, present, or future of a person or a place or a situation with seeming ease. Not all have this clairvoyance, but nearly all spirits evidence some sort of extraordinary mental abilities of this type. Almost all can affect the sleep or dreams of human beings, and even affect the emotional state of fully awake humans, but very few can affect the physical environment that humans inhabit with the same ease humans can with their hands. The most powerful spirits can affect things in a profound way, in ways we can't imagine, but seldom do so, (if they ever do) for a variety of unknown reasons.

III. Allies in the Unseen, Influence and Sorcery

I discuss the mystical ways of spirits because in my conjury, I engage spiritual allies to affect my work and my art. The work to gain the attentions of a spiritual being and to create and maintain the relationship with it is a hard path, but full of rewards. No person more than a spirit can give you guidance and teaching about the realities of this world and the unseen world, as they have many ranges of experience and knowledge that humans do not have. They can also offer great protection that simple charms can't. Also, most divination methods don't achieve their true promise and potency unless spirits are guiding and informing the process.

But at this point, it is important to note that Hoodoo or southern folk-magic (like many other forms of natural magic) does not require an ally in the spirit-world to work. Hoodoo posits the truth that natural objects, forces, and substances have their own innate power. This is beyond a doubt; without the aid of any spirit, certain stones, herbs, candles, prayers, and intentions will exert an influence on the world, and that influence will play a role in how events come to pass in this world.

But beyond simple influence lies real sorcery - if one were to bring the attentions and activities of a powerful spirit or spirits to join with the influence of substance, a great wall of force and power is added to the work. For most people, hoodoo spells and charms work through influence only. And that is fine; it's better to have knowledge of subtle influences and to bring them into your life, than to not have them. It is still a worthy art and collection of lore. It is very much a part of the south, and the swamps and woods.

For some, however, hoodoo truly becomes conjury - the conjuration of spiritual powers to bring their aid and make charms become batteries of power that are animated by spirit allies. And the addition of sorcery to hoodoo is not a new thing; in the old days, spirit-workers were the conjure folk, they were the origin of the famous and well-known recipes and charms that create the corpus of works like Hyatt's masterful collection, and which are known in folklore. You can be certain that spiritual entities gave humans the knowledge of these things, originally.

Since this book is called my "record of operations and technique", I'll be describing my own way of working these things, and that way involves spiritual powers, non-human persons, who bring much power to my work. In my last essay, to follow this one, I will discuss the traditional herb and natural component-driven aspect of hoodoo and southern folk magic, but in my personal work, I make it a point to interweave aspects of spirit contact and worship with the whole.

IV. Spirit Talking

Nearly all of my personal work involves three herbs: sagebrush, sweetgrass, and cedar. I call them my "chief herbs", and they have facilitated for me, over the course of years, powerful gifts and advantages. If I had to name a fourth, it would be tobacco - sweet, fragrant tobacco is one of the chief "offerings" that all spirits adore. Before I describe how I have benefited from the power of these plant-entities, let me remind any of you that might seek them out as allies that these plant-beings are persons themselves, and must be treated with respect. Even cut away from their roots, dried, or prepared in some other manner, they are connected to their sacred origin, and they mediate its power.

Sagebrush - Artemisia tridentata - which is distinct from the Sage plant- has been used by the Native peoples of this continent since time out of mind for purification and blessing. Burned, it produces a powerful and bitter odor, and cleanses of spiritual pollution any person, place, or thing that its smoke wafts over or around. Even though its smoke can be used as an offering to attract spirits, I seldom use it for that. I use it to keep wicked spirits away, to cleanse myself and my working areas and home of spiritual dullness and taint, and to lift my spirits. Wicked spirits are driven away by it, just as surely as negative atmospheres and subtle pollutions are. Even when not burned, sagebrush leaves are good to stuff into mojo bags or conjure bags intended to protect and keep pure people or places. Hung in the house, sagebrush bundles are also protective.

When I get new bundles of sagebrush, I light a new candle and rattle for them - an offering of the shrill rattle-chitter's power to "wake it up", and give it clean, pure water in a bowl to slake its thirst. I talk to it- thanking it for its power and help, and promising to keep a grateful heart, and never throw away its parts into garbage cans. Any part that has to be disposed of is either burned or put outside on the ground. I keep the bundles either hanging on display in a special place, or wrapped safely and in a clean drawer, a box of other powerful things, or a tidy cabinet. This criteria can be used for any herbal bundle that you intend to use in a relationship of power. It also goes for non-corporeal spirits; simple respect and good treatment is what spirits want, the same as human beings. The wise and polite conjure-folk give it.

Sweetgrass - Hierochloe odorata - is the true attractor and food of kindly and helpful spirits, and most spirits otherwise. It is almost universally used in the Americas by the Native peoples for attracting good spirits, and being an offering for them, a meal of sweet power. Burned for spirits, it emits a very pleasing odor and creates a feast of life force for them to partake of. It has a minor purifying power, too, but its chief use is for attracting and feeding goodly powers and spirits.

The evergreen needle-like leaves of Cedar are, like sage, burned to purify and protect, but it also releases a lovely odor and attracts spiritual powers. I find it has the greatest strength when burned alongside sweetgrass. The leaves are great for stuffing into conjure bags or talismans to keep nightmares away from people. A Cedar stick carved into three prongs at one end is a potent anti-evil talisman, and stuck in the ground around your home, they make a powerful barrier.

Shortly put, in nearly all my work, I purify myself and the place where I work in sagebrush smoke, and offer cedar and sweetgrass smoke for Hibou- my helping spirit- and all other powers I wish to gain the aid of. These aren't the only herbs or gifts I use to entice powers, but they are the three main ones, the ones I'd feel lost without, and the ones that ride around with me in a special bag when I travel.

I have a rattle that I made myself. When it comes to instruments of this sort of work, I always suggest that people make their own, though if you can find a local craftsman/artisan who does excellent work by hand, purchasing a rattle or a drum from them is good, too. Rattles and drums create power through sound, and that power can be offered to spiritual powers, as well as affecting the subtle body of the conjure man or woman. Like all people, I have a serpent up and down my back, my spine - but it is also a tree trunk, running from my own roots to my crown.

If my body were to be a channel for spiritual power, along with my mind, my central channel would be my spine. That serpent, that trunk, it aims to the sky and points into the deep earth below. I consider it a superhighway of power, and I know that it can open above and below, joining a person both in mind and in "feeling" to the unseen reaches above and below. "Above and below" are words that refer both to places where spiritual powers dwell, but also metaphors for ranges of consciousness beyond the ordinary consciousness we all live in.

These sorts of explanations are fine and well, but truly, I don't give a rat's ass about expressing things in this manner. There's a trunk in me, a passage, a river-valley, a hollow bone, a serpent, that touches the heights and the depths, and I am where they come together. When I shake my rattle in front of my chest and move it up and down, in front of my face, down to my gut, I feel the tree trunk in me shaking and getting agitated and waking up. I feel bigger and deeper, feel connected. I feel like I can speak to spirits more clearly. And so, I don't question it. Drums can shake up the subtle body too, thundering a person's whole inner body open, knocking open all its hidden doors. You have to fall into the noise, let it penetrate you.

I just do it. And that is just one half of my formula for becoming capable of "contacting spirits" - the real secret is the greater serpent, which I have already discussed at length in my last essay. If you want to contact a spirit, there's something far more important than initial rattling and drumming and herb-burning and carrying on. You just have to shape-shift into a snake, and snake your way into the spirit. Your true body is, after all, a flowing power that is in all other powers, changing them, and being changed by them in return. You can seek out any spirit you need.

Going to seek the spirit - or shimmying to it, or slithering to it - is one thing. Sometimes, you have to do that. But if you're cunning enough, you can attract a spirit. Using its signs or symbols, gathering substances special to it, burning offerings and giving offerings, sending sounds like rattling or drumming to it, and speaking words of power for it- "sending a voice", as it were, you can get it to come to you, perceptually. But even when it comes, it comes on the back of that serpent that is our true power, entwined in all other things.

It's good to start small. Go to the trunk of a nearby tree, and snake into the tree. It's simple when your mind changes into the serpentine flow, and you just go into it, and take it into you. The tree is just one way the non-human spirit person appears, or perhaps one place it lives. It's a symbol all its own. Really, everything's a symbol, and yet, everything isn't. Everything just is what it is- a precious power, a sacred power, a mystery. A kin being, a kin form, a possible friend, foe, or helper, a member of our great spirit-community.

So, when I said "start small", of course that was a joke, even if it wasn't a very funny one. There is no such thing as "small" - even a grain of sand snakes with power through every other form in existence. It's all quite infinite. When you make it "in", reach into power and the unseen, nothing's very small anymore. And yet, it doesn't do to call it all "huge". It just is what it is - beyond finitude.

You can experience the tree (to go with my original example) as a non-human person; you can experience the tree in its non-ordinary way or aspect. This sort of communion begins with a massive expansion of your awareness regarding your intimate relationship to the tree/person, and then becomes a "joining" at the heart level, in which you feel the tree/person, receive strange, wordless messages from it, or become aware of it in some new way. It may influence your dreams, or other phenomenon may occur, "inside" you or "outside" of you.

When "sending voices" to spiritual beings, I find that they enjoy it when you explain yourself. If you're burning sweetgrass for a spirit, tell it what you're doing. When rattling or beating a drum, or making a fire for it, tell it, demonstrate to it the reason for your actions. After you've done this for the same spirit on multiple occasions, you can remind it that it knows what you're doing; "you've seen this before..." This builds up a sequence of power over time.

I have advantages that some reading this may not have if they try to go out, change into a snake, and slide their way into other powers. I have a helping spirit who empowers me to do these things, and so the mental and spiritual changes that come over me, and are subjectively experienced by me, are of a different character. This is why it is important for those who wish to really get into conjury to obtain allies and keep them well related to you by constant repetition of gifts, voice-sending, and the creation of artistic representations of them, which you should keep in your living place, where you can see them all the time. When your mind sees these things, you build up the channel they use. Even in that simple practice, you invisibly snake into them, and them into you. If you get lax in your daily "bonding", you gradually begin to lose the connection and the power. For me, the real secret to "snaking" into and out of things begins with the strong commitment to being mentally flexible and being alert - very aware of everything that arises in your senses. From that basic condition of "openness", one adds the sorcerously inspired imagination and the knowledge - the certain knowledge - that the powers which make up our bodies and minds are of the same nature as all the "other" powers outside us. When you make the leap to connect the earth of your flesh to the earth under your feet, you slide into an "open space" where you aren't so separate anymore. If you let yourself go, you can "fall" into the earth, really experience yourself as part of it. This is true for any power.

The last element is, of course, sorcerous excitement and a touch of love for the art, and affection for the powers that make up the totality of our world and your true body. If you aren't excited by this art, you won't go far.

V. Five Guidelines to Spirit-Speaking

The following five guidelines have been invaluable to me in my quest to gain actual contact with non-human persons. I will explain each after you read them.

1. Gaining proximity to a phenomenon related to the non-human person you wish to engage in direct communication with

2. Cultivating a sense of the non-humanness of this spirit or person

3. Cultivating a respectful attitude and heart towards this spirit or person

4. Formally gaining the attention of the spirit person

5. Going into a passive mode of openness.

Basically put, you should try to "gain closeness" to some phenomenon that is tied into the spirit-person that you wish contact with. For a spirit like the Earth-Mother herself, or even Gran Ibo, the Old Woman of the Swamp, just being on the earth or in a swamp puts you close. Of course, drawing special symbols or signs that represent these powers also puts you close. Collecting other things that are tied into them and using them in a rite, puts you close. Try your best to get as "close" to the non-human person as you can.

It is very important that you do your best to let the non-human person be a non-human person. This is what most today don't do; especially the youthful new-age sector. They want spirits to be very human-like, but spirits are not humans. You have to extend both respect to the spirit, by letting it be as strange-seeming or unpredictable as it will be, and you have to extend flexibility. Don't try to imagine what the spirit is or what it will be like at the time of your work.

More respect must be extended, thirdly; you must always bring a heart of real respect for the personhood of the spirit. The stage of "formally getting the attention" of a spirit is when you make your voice-sendings, your sound-sendings, your gifts, and the like.

Last is the most important step, to me. Going passive and open to whatever the spirit may reveal to you, or make you see or feel. To this final step, something crucial must be added: spirits may not come and talk to you or join with you at all, no matter how well your rite for them was, or how excited or hopeful you are. That is their right; you must accord them the right to not speak to you on any given occasion. They have that right, as they are sovereign beings all on their own. Most people get upset when their attempts at spirit-contact don't "work"- but this is the most disrespectful thing of all. You must not be obsessed with any certain outcome, and you must always be respectful.

VI. Getting Over There:
Ghost-going and Making Things Two-Headed

Sometimes, we don't attract spirits to us and our places of business; sometimes, we go to theirs. On the back of the serpent, you can flow both ways, or go anywhere. The benefit of going to a spirit's home is that you can have a deeper experience of it; this is especially important when you need to have a full-blown conversational experience of the spirit. This is very much like "going for a visit", and it requires from you the same sort of respect you'd have if you went to a human friend's house for a visit.

Trance-going, or ghost-going, requires you to change yourself - to change your condition of mind and body, so that you can slide away into the unseen. Likely enough, spirits have to change their conditions of mind and whatever strange bodies they have to get "close" to us, so this practice is really a fair reciprocity as well as a powerful, universal experience found in all primal human cultures.

To entrance and shed the skin, to spirit-step somewhere, slither somewhere like a ghost, one must understand and accept that they are about to actually move their mind and part of their spirit or soul into an unseen world. There can be no pussy-footing around this fact; none of this "the unseen world is just another way of saying our unconscious mind" or "collective unconscious" nonsense. I'm not saying that there isn't a relationship between the unseen and the unconscious land of the human self, just that this isn't a Jungian psychology class or activity. This is travel into the world of the Invisibles. Your mind must be oriented towards this as a fact, before it can go.

To "get over there", one has to find a way "down". If you live in swampy land, you're surrounded by nothing but massive ways "down" - any marshy, swampy land is a natural entrance into the unseen. There is always a sense of going down - of sinking down to a deep place - when you want to go over to the unseen. Some people imagine that it will be a "going sideways" - like through a door on the same horizontal plane - or going up, even; but in my practice, and in keeping with the work of years of anthropological research regarding the use of lower world passages by shamans in various societies, I always end up "slithering down", to a perceptual layer of reality that appears to be below this world. It is a complete other reality, every bit as real as this one, and related to this one, tied together with this one, in many ways.

One of the ways it ties into this one is through the human mind. Another way is through tunnels, caves, wells, animal dens, natural deep holes in the ground, marshes, swamps, lakes, rivers, trees with big root-systems, and bogs. The act of going low forces the mind into a new mode of perception; this is the key to the entire sorcerous act.

To spirit-step, one must find their place, their ghost-hole, their entry point. Then, one must go into a room or enclosure, lit only by candlelight or no light at all, and tie a dark cloth over their eyes, and lie down flat on their back. When lying in this manner, one must relax the body with long deep breaths - but breaths that come out in a slow hissing whisper. You are going to become the snake that slithers down a deep hole into the world below. While lying there, relaxing, imagine that your arms and legs disappear into your body, leaving a serpent's body there, heavy and dull and relaxing. You should always burn sagebrush over yourself and the area you'll be laying in, before you do this. I find that it helps enormously to pray to the Old One, the Master of Crossroads who controls passage between the seen and the unseen, to let you cross quickly and safely, and return quickly and safely..

Most people today who undergo this "lower world regression" use drums - and there is a reason. at **180** beats per minute, the deep sound of a drum (and it has to be a lower sounding drum) matches the song that the ground or earth itself is making at all times. If someone is in the room with you drumming, have them drum at that steady rate. If you're alone, you can go without the physical drum, instead letting yourself re-create the noise from your memory and imagination, or use a recording with headphones.

After you've made your body into the lazy serpent lying there, and hissed yourself into deep relaxation, and are in total darkness due to the black eye band, let the drum sound rise to blast through you and tear you away. You have to let the sound take you away, like a horse racing off, a wave of sound that you surrender to, and become part of the motion of. You become the sound, snake into the sound, and it is a sound of energy and moving, of motion.

When you fall into this enough, and lose the distinction between yourself and it, your brain and soul will be in sync with the ground, with the great changing power. At that special point, that point of partial self-loss, but strong awareness, let your mind's eye see the entry point you have chosen. Go into it, and fly down, being pushed by the sound, however you are having the sound provided. And then, in the darkness below your entry point, keep going, down, down, down as though you are flying down many miles into darkness.

A point will come when you find that "something" feels like it is approaching you, coming to meet your face. Some people see tunnels under their entry points, and others just see dark voids- that really doesn't matter, so long as you can hold the vision of moving downwards. As the strange power comes up to you, what is happening is that you are reaching the deep layer, the entrance to the underworld. Don't ever hurry this process - let it unfold as it will. It also helps if you perform this act as close to your entry point as possible.

When you go through the "bottom", you will find yourself in a wild, strange world where visions and strange shapes and dreams and objects swirl about, without making much sense. It's very much like being in a waking dream. Sometimes it may seem like a regular landscape, like a forest or a bog or even a town or city. It's never predictable. Don't try to decide what it should look like or what you should see. Go with whatever appears first.

You will feel dull, distant from yourself, deeply entranced, perhaps even unable to feel your heart beating or feel your own breathing. You may not feel your body at all. That's disconcerting, but fine, and a sign of good power and separation. What's more important is the visions that will be greeting you. You can now work in the lower state, sending voices, or even rattling or drumming, as you have a mental body, and the power to shape-shift very easily. You can call on the spirit you're looking for, or ask other powers you see to take you to it; you'd have to be respectful, of course, and offer them gifts, gifts that you can summon - or make promises that you will burn and offer things to them when you return if they help you. Don't even think of not living up to your word!

You can wander about a bit, but it is always better not to wander too far. If some power or being frightens you or seems threatening, avoid it and get away from it. If it persists in bothering you, fly back up instantly, in the speed of a lightning flash, and come back to your body and get up, move around, burn more sagebrush over yourself and the area and go have a hot meal. Try again later. As a general rule, don't do this practice more than four or five times a week, if you can help it. Four or five times would be a lot. Never do this spirit-going work for frivolous reasons.

Eventually, in your moving about in the world of the invisibles, you'll find your way to the spirit you're looking for, and you'll find them easier if you tell them you're coming the night before you go, and make offerings and drum and rattle for them and send voices for them. It's polite to ask if you can come, and to ask them to help you by being near you when you emerge below.

This technique, if carried through, gets you into a visionary state in which you can talk directly to spirits, as they appear to your mind's eye. They can appear as nearly anything. You can't let yourself expect them to appear one way or another. Often, they don't speak back to you, to answer questions; they move in certain ways, or make things appear, or lead you somewhere, through the spectral landscape, to show you things, to make answers for you. If a spirit gives you something, or wants to go with you or come back with you or enter you, then pull the thing it gives, or the spirit itself, into your chest, hold it there, and fly back up with it to your entranced body.

As soon as you arrive back with it, or with something, stand up and rattle or drum yourself, and speak out loud what happened. Draw images of what you saw - this is important, and it doesn't matter how crude the images are. You have to integrate the invisible experience with the world that is visible, make the experience "have two heads" - the "head" of what it was in the invisible, and the "head" that can be seen in this world - because this brings the two worlds together and bridges the power over, making it whole and manifest.

If the spirit itself is in you, integrated with your mind and body, then dance it - move around, in a steady rhythm, and put your own mind and person "aside" - let the spirit express itself through you however it likes. Just let go, and let it become dominant. This is not a hard thing to do; you will feel it in your chest, and it will rise up further, to your head and throat. Imagine what it would be like being that sort of spirit, and just let your limbs and mouth move without thinking about it.

This spirit dancing is quite powerful, as it forges connections between you and this spirit, which will be eager to help you in the future if you offer to let it live as you again. The dance ends naturally on its own, with the spirit either receding back into your chest, or vanishing off entirely.

If you are integrating a power or a thing that the spirit gave you, either create an image of it on paper, or a model or symbolic representation of it somehow, and breathe the power from your chest into the physical thing you made. A bundle is a good thing to make, to capture some of the power. Don't breathe it all; leave some in you, but give some to the "thing" out here, in this world.

Your body, when your chest is full of some power, becomes the real talisman or fetish. Two worlds come together in you, and sometimes, two persons become one in you.

VII. Laying Tricks: Making the Invisible Become Visible

These guides and criteria I've been giving all have the same use: to either coax powers to come and help you "lay tricks" or make conjure-bags, or just aid you in workings. Sometimes, you'll sink on down to a spirit because you want advice, a vision of divination, or an answer to a hard question. Sometimes, you'll spirit-step to gain a power you need for a practical work, and bring it back to integrate with your work.

Whether you've attracted a spirit or a power, or gone and gotten a power from a spirit, the secret to getting it "into" your work is simple enough; burn cedar and sweetgrass, or some other incense especially prepared for the work, and...

-If you attracted a spirit, offer that smoke to them, and then, blow the smoke over the object of the work, such as a conjure-bag, a doll, a photo, a drawing, a representation, a bundle, or whatever it is you are working with;

-If you gained a power within yourself from a spirit, blow the power from inside your chest into the smoke and force the smoke (now carrying the power) to rush over the object of your work.

Of course, you are always telling the spirit why you attracted it- telling it what you're doing and why you need its help. If it's just a power you have inside your chest, you don't have to explain anything, just send it over there with the smoke. If you're giving the spirits food to eat or something to drink, you can rub or sprinkle the object of your work with a portion of that, too.

The unseen becomes "seen" when you send it into a physical thing. Also, drawing what you saw, speaking out-loud what you saw and experienced - these words of power are natural ways to make the unseen a thing of this world. Bring the worlds together - that is the key. Make the power "lay down" on the object of your work, and they will bring great force to it.

VIII: Old Man That Scarecrow

Scarecrows are objects that scare away evil or harmful spirits. They can be anything, but in South Louisiana, Alligator heads are common. I use the skulls of antlered or horned animals, because antlers and horns are signs of attack and threat in the animal world, signs of might. And, let's face it - skulls are scary, in a way. And this is important. But a scarecrow can be anything; a literal "doll" stuffed with Spanish moss and painted with a terrifying face will do the trick, too. The secret is to make them powerful with either a spirit you attract to empower them in their scarecrow-force, or to gain a power through spirit-stepping, and pass that power into the scarecrow.

I recently slid on down and met Hibou, who took the form of a woman in a classroom, in an old school. I had asked him to show me a sign or symbol that would terrify evil spirits, and so, in that trance-vision, she sketched that symbol on the blackboard for me. I memorized it and flew back, and immediately drew what I had seen- made the invisible visible. You can feel the power when you bring the two worlds together.

That symbol is painted by me in a mixture of red ochre, blood, linseed oil, and certain other powders, onto a antlered skull I have, and it hangs over my working area. It also protects my house in this way. Any spirit of sufficient power can show you a symbol that will do the same. I'd keep that symbol to yourself, if I were you. You have to have some things private, unique to your practice.

IX. Visible Work and Invisible Work

Sometimes - oftentimes - you bring many things together for your work. You collect herbs, write parchments, get special stones or earth or water; and you get candles, or incenses, and you make bundles, bags, or bottles full of components. You may drum or chant or rattle or any combination of things. There is no one formula; you must do what works, what brings together the serpentine tapestry of power in line with what you're trying to do.

I call this "visible work" - it's planned out, artful, and quite powerful, if it succeeds. Many influences are brought to bear. Sometimes, spirits come to add their force to it. But there is another sort of work, and it is the sort that will sometimes happen to you without you meaning for it to - invisible work. I've mentioned it before, but it bears being mentioned again. Sometimes, you'll find yourself gripped by a power, and guided, without knowing why or how, to do certain things.

Spontaneous, unplanned work is invisible work - and it is the most powerful kind, I find. You'll just grab certain components or things, speak weird sentences or shake rattles, perform a spontaneous spirit-stepping, and do all manner of strangeness, but it always serves some goal or function in your life and work. You'll have this invisible work happen with more frequency the closer you get to the world of the invisibles.

X. Laying like a Corpse and The Great Darkness

Laying Like a Corpse means laying down in a dark room, again on your back, and going silent and still. Close your eyes, and get quiet and go still. Lay like you're a dead body. Don't think one thing or another, and if thoughts come, just let them slide away. Corpses don't think, after all.

Something strange begins to happen, if you let yourself go into silence and stillness, and you endure this hardship. Motion and noise that you will still comprehend around you, even distantly, start to seem very strange. Even the motion of your thoughts become disassociated from some "other" part of you. The great darkness that is the true origin of things is silent and still, too. When you become silent and still, you start to "go into" it - and you start to see how noise and motion are really resolved into silence and stillness, which is maybe all they really are, just with a twist. You begin to feel like a bit of moss on the tip of a planet-sized iceberg, floating in a great brackish sea. A "great divide" starts to happen.

This sounds esoteric, and for good reasons. This divine reality begins to seep up into your awareness. You begin to feel alien, like your thoughts and feelings are just surface crust over something immense, dark, eternal, ancient, and young, or just infinite. It hurts, doing this practice, sometimes, because you want to move and make noise, but if you let yourself be just dead enough - truly imagine that you are a corpse that can't move or think or feel - then your thoughts and feelings and everything else separates away from you, eventually.

You may have to lay there a long time. But eventually, you come face to face with something amazing. You can't fall asleep while doing this, so make sure you have enough energy when you lie down.

That "something amazing" you come face to face with will be more feelings and thoughts of utter amazement. Then, you even have to let those go, because they are still motion and mind-noise, not the great darkness. No particular "state" or "thing" you experience is the great darkness, and the practice of letting even experiences of wonder and peace and infinity fall off you into it, purifying yourself further, is what this is really about.

People sometimes say "all is one", but that statement must be placed in proper context and understanding. Everything is arising from the great darkness. Something vast and mysterious intends for things to appear a certain way, I believe. That something vast and mysterious is power, and every experience you have is a pattern of power. Persons are patterns of power that have become conscious. Things aren't just one thing - things are things - but all are in one great unified family of existence.

If you keep this "Laying like a Corpse" practice up, you'll become truly empty and beyond life and death. This is something beyond description, but when you come "back" from it - and it takes months of practice, sometimes - you'll notice two things.

1. That things begin to happen in your life in helpful ways. You begin to understand your life better, begin to recognize signs in your life that guide you, and you feel more at peace. Your conjure work will also increase in power.

2. That you can begin to sense the great darkness and stillness and silence "behind and within" everything, even in the midst of noise and commotion.

These things are very important, for many reasons. They are the goals of many a wise person throughout history - and the experience of disassociation and seeing the great darkness is something near to what the dead have to experience at the time of death. These insights are keys to a power that puts a human being in the company of powerful spirits. This is the most esoteric aspect of my work, hard to explain to others, but not one that I'd ever give up. I suggest doing it about once a week, or so. Sometimes twice a week. But you have to go as long as you can with this Corpse Laying, each session, no matter how hard it is. It also helps to burn sagebrush and wrap your head in a white cloth before you do it. It also helps to do it after bathing and purifying in bathwater.

Part IV:
Charms, Tricks, and Lores

"The whiskey you bought me, I was afraid to unscrew it,
The Gypsy woman told me it was embalming fluid
You got a Black Cat Bone and a Buzzard Feather,
A John the Conquer Root and they're all tied together"
                                                    -Esmond Edwards

I. House of Flesh: The Sorcerous Apothecary

A Conjure Man or Woman looks to the vast storehouse of natural substances all around for the bones and blood of their art. I tend to divide conjury between the Spirit House and the Flesh House - which are not, as it may seem, terms of some philosophical dualistic division, but words that point to the operations of subtle contact and intangible things (such as speaking to spirits and obtaining their aid) and the operations involving plants, resins, dusts, waters, and oils, as well as the body parts of animals and people.

Every great operation of conjury really involves the powers of both houses. The awesome and unseen powers of the spirit world gain their greatest ability to affect this world when their force is summoned and grounded in the things of this world, so these two houses are two halves of a singular power-flow, a singular operating process. I have discussed the operations of spirit at length; now I must discuss notes and criteria for the "other side", the side more often recognized as hoodoo and mojo-working.

This voyage into the House of Flesh takes us into the literal flesh of the world - the land's hairs and skin, the mosses, plants, stones, and dirt that is all around us - and all of which are patterns of power, sacred and potent, with influences that can and do affect the world and its living beings at all times. Anyone who is aware of their surroundings at a slightly deeper level than others can feel the subtle influence of the land beneath their feet - they know what sorts of hidden communications are going on between the land and the people on it, at all times.

You can belong to a place, be as much a part of it as local trees or rivers. You learn this through trance, through having a mystical, open heart, or through something as mundane as moving far away from the place that "has" you. One day, after your move, you'll begin feeling the tug of your parent-land, and dreams will come. Urges below the surface will move you; this can sometimes be mistaken for "homesickness", but for those sufficiently aware, it is more: it is part of a living system of communication and power-sharing.

Being a part of your land means being a part of a greater whole, and it means being part of a broad family of living beings, of human and non-human persons. The rivers, lakes, swamps, flowers, herbs, and animals of your land are the non-human persons that join you in existing there. Sometimes your power helps them or harms them; sometimes, their powers help you or harm you. There is a spiritual ecology here that can never be ignored by a root-worker or a conjure-man. There is also a need to know where the land "has" you, because this is no trap; this is the land telling you where your real power is.

When you know your place, and recognize your membership in the family of powers and persons, you are truly ready to begin collecting about yourself your own root-shack or mojo-house, your own sorcerous apothecary or collection of items and substances of power, from which you will draw the materials needed for your conjury. Power-workers and mystics of natural and animistic traditions from all places and ages have gathered the substances of the land around them to aid them in their work; this practice is nothing new. The act of collecting substances and materials from the land is another expression of bonding with the land. The land will give you all you need; what you need to receive it is awareness- to be perfectly open to what's occurring.

You have to keep an eye open to what is near and around and below. The greatest components of the conjury art are often the things people overlook the most - the plant (sometimes described as a "weed") growing out of the side of a hedge, the bones laying in the dirt off the side of the road, and the scattering of fallen feathers off of the side of a trail. Most people will overlook these things quickly, but to a person in touch with something greater, they can be signs and they can be objects of power.

Creating an apothecary or a botanica or a collection of powerful substances of any kind is a natural initiatory rite of passage. It dramatically increases one's ability to affect the world, and establishes one in a new identity; one goes from being a sorcerer alone to a sorcerer who runs a house of powers, who has many allies and friends.

Before a person can be the true master of a house, they have to be a master of certain lores and knowledge. Herbal lore, wortcunning, and the craft of extracting the medicinal and sorcerous constituents of herbs and preserving them in oil or fluid form is needed. the knowledge of drying herbs, of storing them, of growing them and collecting them, of identifying them and their many uses in alleviating human sickness and discomfort, is all necessary. This is likely the oldest of sorcerous arts, after the art of spirit-talking, and it was spirits that taught the first human herbalists and healers their craft. Not all conjure folk will be healers with herbs, but most will have some knowledge of uses for herbs beyond that of just sorcery.

For the "pure sorcerers" out there, herbal knowledge and substance knowledge will be largely magical. But in my time of dealing with these sacred things, my knowledge-base has always grown together: the medicinal uses of things and the magical seem to grow together, play off of one another, and compliment one another. Conjury is about changing things, about the constant reality of sorcerous change, and how it is entwined with substances and activities. If you can bring about a healing change in someone's sleep problems with an infusion of valerian easier than you can with a mojo-bag for rest or peaceful sleep, you probably should. It never hurts to know more than one way to change things.

In times past, herbal wisdom and cunning was hard to find and learn; you either learned it from your family through fortune of birth into a wise family, or you sought out a teacher, who could be costly or hard to find. Today, we have access to astounding ranges of herbal knowledge, bound for us in excellent books. Nothing should stop a person who is either beginning or at the intermediate stage of their conjure-art from obtaining as many herbals and other information books about the identification and medicinal uses of herbs and plants as they can. For those sorcerously inclined, there are books specifically written regarding the use of plants and substances for magical arts - and for those with an interest in Hoodoo, I can offer no better a suggestion than "Hoodoo Herb and Root Magic" by Catherine Yronwode.

Yronwode draws her massive knowledge base of Hoodoo from the Hyatt corpus, a superb and massive collection (723 pages alone in his work "Folk-Lore From Adams County Illinois") of folklore and hoodoo information done in the early part of the twentieth century, and considered the most authoritative written source for Hoodoo knowledge. Despite what some have said, it is not flawed or invented; it is a solid ethnographical and anthropologically sound body of work, filled with information taken first hand from living people with traditional Hoodoo knowledge.

A person should learn from the book sources, learn from practice, learn from people you meet, learn from informants. Collect power, collect substances, collect knowledge. Hoodoo and Conjury draw from many sources, Native American, European, and African. There are many excellent sources of Native American herb-lore, and the finest I know is one of the smallest and least-known: "Micmac Medicines" by Laurie Lacey. The Micmac Indians were inter-married with and mentors to the Acadian people, who after diaspora became the Cajuns of South Louisiana, so there is a historical link between the natural lores of the Micmacs and the herbal lores of the Cajun people.

Part of gaining herbal knowledge is knowing what herbs to collect and store in various forms for your apothecary or root-hut, for the most common sorcerous and medicinal uses. There are many ways to know what things plants influence or what they "do" when employed in an extraordinary way. Some cunning people look to the "seven planetary currents" for a basic system born in European folklore, and I have found this system to be evergreen and useful.

I give now a short, poetic description of the associations of the seven planetary currents of sorcerous power and how they entwine within the world of plants and threes:

There are the astral, dreamy, deceptive, and psychism-inducing lunar herbs like willow, lily, acacia, myrrh, jasmine, lemon, and mugwort; the divination-aiding, communication-strengthening and sorcery-increasing mercurial herbs like peppermint, dill, ash, morning glory, poppy, and sage; the lustful, fertile, love-binding, and beguiling venusian herbs like rose, rosemary, marigold, lady's mantle, honeysuckle, vervain, coriander, apple and birch; the healing, helping, and honor-bestowing solar herbs like hypercium, angelica, cinnamon, rowan, chamomile, saffron, frankincense, and daisy.

This list continues, along traditional lines: we have the wrathful-curse creating, strength-increasing, evil-spirit exorcising and masculine martial herbs like onion, pine, wormwood, rue, black and red peppers, ginger, peppercorns, holly, and garlic; the authoritative, fertile, wealth-increasing, protective jupiterian herbs like houseleek, hyssop, oak, borage, figs, cloves, nutmeg, maple, and sagebrush; and the cold-curse creating, deathly, will-binding, occult-knowledge increasing saturnian herbs - saturnian herbs which also see to the well-being of home and land - like nightshade, datura, foxglove, elder, cypress, mullein, juniper, hemp, hellebore, and valerian.

This is one rudimentary yet useful, working system. Anyone in possession of Hoodoo Herb and Root Magic will see another, one more aligned to the mainstream tradition of Hoodoo. It gives exhaustive lists of sorcerous goals and motivations (luck, blessing, crossing, spirit-contact, uncrossing, etc.) and what plants and other natural substances were held by traditional root-workers and conjure folk to have influence and power over those things.

One can create a useful list of herbs to obtain and preserve from looking to that work, just as one can gain an idea of what herbs to obtain from the sevenfold list I gave above. Some of the traditional and very useful roots and herbs of Hoodoo are not on that list, but surely you know them by now - Hyssop, which purifies you if you bathe in it; High John the Conquer root, which gives luck in games of chance and business, but also makes sure that you're never long without money, a lover, or personal strength; Low John or Little John to Chew, which gives you luck in court, but can be chewed and spit out to break curses and jinxes, or turn away enemies; Dixie John, for luck, sex appeal, and protection of relationships; Salep Root, for making love and gambling spells stronger; and Buckeye Nuts, to ward off headaches and make a man virile - to name a few. Get your hands on them.

II. Some Key Components

Along with whatever plants and substances you intend to find or somehow obtain, I have compiled a list of items and substances that will serve you greatly in your work. Before I give it, understand that any and all of the tools of an herbalist are necessary - strainers, droppers, filters, funnels, the ever-important mortar and pestle, non-aluminum pots, and measuring cups and spoons. For stirring boiling mixtures, I prefer to use wooden spoons.

Before I continue on with this listing, understand that some of the plants you will want to obtain cannot always be found near you, or be obtained in the best way, which is finding them in the wild or growing them yourself and respectfully taking the parts you need. There are merchants who supply people with excellent plant-parts - either fresh, dried, or seeds of plants - or even whole plants shipped live to you. Find reliable merchants of this kind and keep their contact information near and dear to you. Utilize them.

As for the other things you should accumulate, I find that sunflower oil, grapeseed oil, and almond oil make the best and most neutral "light" oils for creating herbal oils, which I will discuss in detail soon. Candles of every size and color tend to be useful, but as I will discuss soon, true old time hoodoo and conjury was born in an era when colored candles didn't really exist, beyond the colors of white, tallow brown, beeswax tan or brown, and sometimes black. White candles can be used for nearly anything, and are to be preferred; and I find that red and black make the next most useful colors to keep around, as red has a minor "general" use, being the closest to the old fashioned brown, and a symbol of magical power (red is power, but also passion) and black for jinxing and crossing. Don't hesitate to get natural colored beeswax and tallow candles, if you can find them.

Sulphur powder is used in many dusts and powders, but also in mojo bags, specifically associated with darker operations. Graveyard dirt, despite its name, is used for many operations, not just conjury of harm or crossing, as will be described below in great detail. Ammonia has (in places) come to replace urine in hoodoo works, but also has its own use as a general sorcerous cleaner and purifier, and has many uses. Urine is also used too, but hardly needs to be collected; any healthy person produces an abundance of it daily. The skin of snakes and bones or other parts thereof are also to be collected if you can get them; they have their own special uses in the art, especially when powdered, and especially (for bane workings) when it's a rattlesnake.

Salts - regular Salt and Epsom Salt - should be obtained and put aside for works of hoodoo; by themselves they are for purification, sanctification, and protection, but Epsom salts in combination with other substances can be used even for jinxing. Rum and Whiskey are both good to have bottled and kept as offerings to spirits and payment to spirits of all kinds, and sometimes for other uses; and Vodka or very strong grain liquors are used to stabilize tinctures - to stop them from going rancid or bad (which we will discuss soon) - and for adding to various waters and washes for purifying power and power in general.

Muslin or cheesecloth should be obtained, for use in straining spent herb-parts and the like from waters, tinctures, decoctions, infusions, and oils, as they are being bottled or poured into containers. Flannel of various colors, especially red, are the traditional cloth for making mojo bags or conjure-bags, but (in line with the organic nature of this tradition) I find that any good natural cloth of quality can be used, such as linen or wool. Leather is also traditional for holding ingredients. Don't sew or tie up these bags with too much fancy or synthetic stuff; I get good, simple natural thin fiber cord, un-dyed and natural in color, natural leather lace, and other such ties and threads for tying up mine. Simpler and more natural is almost always better in every case.

Frankincense is an all-around very powerful purifier and disperser of negativity, when it is burned in resin form on coals. It also has other uses as an ingredient in mojo-bags; it can be added to any bag to simply increase its power.

Jars and bottles and vials are needful, and you should start collecting them. You need to especially accumulate blue glass, amber and dark amber glass, and dark green glass, because many of the oils and waters and tinctures (and the like) you'll make do not take well to sunlight and bright light, and are protected from it behind dark colored glass. Also, these bottles - especially the antique ones - add an amazing ambiance of power to the entire art and craft of conjury.

Mason jars that seal well are to be especially treasured for holding all manner of things. Most jars and containers that need to be stored will be stored in cabinets, or darker, cooler places. Always be sure that you find stoppers or corks that seal tight and well. I prefer rubber myself, but actual cork is traditional. Melted wax can also be used to reinforce a seal, and I find that this is needful when I am forced to use regular cork.

Rust Powder - the scrapings of rust from iron and other metals- is needful for the creation of war water, which we will discuss below, and for adding the martial, strong power to mixtures and even mojo-bags. Corn meal and flour have dozens of uses, as we will cover. Spanish moss is used for the stuffing of the famous "voodoo dolls" or "doll-babies" that have become so sensationalized, and the grim, creepy grey and twisty moss is in fact used for some jinxing work. But not all poppets or dolls are created for negative ends. All doll-babies should contain actual parts of the people they are intended to influence- like fingernail or toenail clippings, hair, and even have the blood, sexual fluids, sweat, or urine from that person incorporated into their cloth, if those things can be obtained. Clothing from the person can be used to make the clothing of the doll-baby.

Of course, for me, this short walk ends with my usual praise of the usefulness of the herbs sagebrush, sweetgrass, and cedar. I wouldn't be complete without them, nor would my conjury be as strong. Nor would I ever be found without fresh tobacco to feed spirits - they treasure it as a food like no other substance, and will work for it the same way human beings will work for cash money.

III. Sorcerous Formulary: Essential Works and Herbal Preparations

In the previous essays, I discussed the manner in which I honor the sagebrush bundles and sweetgrass bundles I obtain from merchants, or the cedar bundles I make from my gatherings from the cedar trees, and how I continually treat them well. This show of respect for the power that they are a part of is important for all herbs, insofar as you can manage it. I find that it makes my workings that much more powerful, and it satisfies my own need to feel respectful and "in my place" in the community of power that is all things. Perhaps my own power stems from keeping that perspective. Others may not; still, I maintain that nearly all powers and substances either are non-human persons in some manner, or connected to and protected by non-human persons, and that respect always wins you more power and effectiveness than not.

Keep fresh herbs wrapped and in airtight jars before their use or preparation. If you're going to dry them, hang them midway up a wall or higher, so that rising heat helps the process. Around **75** degrees is the ideal drying temperature; always keep drying herbs out of direct sunlight, which will damage them and degenerate both their sorcerous and medicinal properties. I like to hang them from horizontal strings, sometimes, or horizontal thin wooden poles. Hanging them like this is better, because air can circulate freely around them.

It takes about a week in these conditions for most to dry, and up to four weeks for the largest and most vivacious leaves and stems. Do not wash leaves or plants before you dry them! Wipe off visible soil, and that's it- making plants too wet gives bacteria an advantage in growing in them and destroying them during preparation.

An airtight jar for storing fresh or even dried herbs is good because moisture in the air is what allows for rot or bacterial infections. I find that putting a dry piece of paper, like a fibrous brown paper, on the bottom of the jar helps because it absorbs any stray moisture that will be in the air of the jar. Store them in a darker, cooler place.

Herbs properly dried and stored will maintain potency for a year (to be safe) to a year and a half (on the outside, it seems.) Fresh herbs that don't get dried or used in some other way do not last longer than a few days.

Drying herbs is the most common way you'll keep them for long-term use, but there are other ways, of course. Creating tinctures and oils are the two best ways to capture the essence of herbs and keep them the longest for use. Making hydrosols or essential waters is a good way of capturing the essence of aromatic herbs, and these can be stabilized by strong, clear liquors or alcohol for long-term storage and use.

Any herbal preparation should be made on the day of the week corresponding to the planetary alignment of the herb, or, if the preparation takes days or weeks to make, it should be started on the planetary day- assuming you know the alignment. If not, do it when it feels right, or when a spirit tells you to.

You create a tincture, or an alcohol-based extract of a plant, chiefly because it is very potent, and stored properly, will last for three years. For many plants, alcohol used as a carrier or solvent will extract a larger range of needful and useful constituents from the plant. Alcohol concentrates the power and acts as a preservative. You can make tinctures from fresh or dried herbs.

I use either **8** ounces of dried herb, or a pound of the fresh herb, and I put it in a large jar. I add three cups of vodka in the jar, and one and a fourth cups of water, and I close the jar tight. You have to keep this jar in a warmish place for two weeks, shaking it well once a day. At the end of that time, you strain the mixture through muslin or cheesecloth, and then take the soaked plant remains and squeeze those through the cloth into the new container that you are straining into. You dispose of the remains, and keep the strained mixture. The tincture has to be kept in a dark glass bottle, and must be kept away from direct sunlight, in a cool place.

Tinctures are great for herbs that have healing or medicinal properties, because you can pass those properties directly into the body by (adults) taking **5** to **20** drops up to three times a day (never exceeding one teaspoon per dose) directly, and (children under **12**) taking **5** to **10** drops daily up to three times a day.

If you don't want the alcohol, you can mix the dose in with some hot water, and the alcohol will evaporate off, leaving just the plant extract. Of course, it goes without saying (and yet here I am saying it) that some plants will have a very high probability of killing you if you take their tinctures even in small doses, so always know your plants and their medicinal uses, and know what's poisonous and what's not.

Any good herbal will tell you of the many remarkable- and easily obtainable- plants that can be used to heal or alleviate an enormous variety of symptoms in people.

IV. The Art of Infused Oils and Working the Waters

Infused oils are another long-lasting and ancient method for storing the power of plants. They are easy to make, and can even be made quickly, if you want to be daring and somewhat more modern in your preparation. Making oils on the basic pattern is simple - you fill a clear glass jar with the fresh herb, and cover them with one of the light vegetable oils I mentioned above, and close the jar up tight, leaving it in a warm, sunlight-filled place for four to six weeks. Shake it a bit, once a day.

After that, strain it, and store it in a dark glass bottle, kept safe from sun or heat. These infused oils last a greatest potency for about six months. This is the most primitive and most traditional way ("the solar method") to make infused oil. Bear in mind that infused oils are not essential oils; essential oils are highly concentrated products of special distillation processes. If you are trying to make an oil from a thick, hard root - like a fresh ginger root - carve it up first; shave it up into a wet pile of shavings before covering it with oil.

If all you have is dried herbs, they can still be use to make an infused oil, but it will be somewhat weaker. One advantage of dried herbs is there's no chance that bacteria from the moisture of the fresh herb will sour the oil or turn it milky. Also, dried herbs will expand in oil over time, so always put some extra oil on top of them to give them room to "grow."

Oils - with fresh or dried herbs - can be heated to speed this process up, in a crock pot or an oven. In an oven, you put the herbs and oil into an oven-safe container, and let them sit in the oven on a very low setting for **2-3** hours, always checking on them to make sure they aren't frying or sizzling. In a crock pot, you let the herbs and oil sit covered in the pot for **3-6** hours on the lowest setting. Strain and store as usual.

Essential waters or herbal waters (hydrosols) are made through distilling the chemical compounds and constituents out of the fresh leaves and flowers of aromatic plants, like roses or rosemary or orange flowers, lavender, mints, thyme, or many others. I find these the most fun to make because making them requires you to build a small still in your home, a stovetop still that extracts the essentials from the plant and condenses it into a fragrant water.

To create the contraption you'll need, you first take a big stock pot which has a curved or slightly round lid, a fireplace brick, as much of the fragrant herb's leaves and flowers and fresh, fragrant parts as you can obtain (a good amount is **2** or **3** quarts), and a bowl, preferably of thick earthenware, but it can be metal so long as it isn't aluminum. Stand the brick up inside the pot, and put the plant parts all around the inside, around the brick. Cover them with water, so that you have a lake in the pot of floating plant parts, with the top third of the brick sticking up out of it, above the water level. Place the bowl on top of the brick, and then put the lid on the pot upside down.

Now, start the fire under the pot, to bring it to a roiling boil. As soon as the water starts to boil, fill the top of the lid on the pot (which is upside down, and therefore shaped like a shallow bowl) with ice cubes.

Then, lower the heat level to make the fluid inside simmer at a steady pace - not too slow, not too high. What you have done is create a still - as the steam rises from the bottom inside of the pot, carrying the chemical constituents, it collides with the freezing cold lid and condenses, dripping down to the center of the lid and dripping into the bowl inside. It is that condensed fluid you want- every twenty minutes or so, take the lid off, steal as many tablespoons of the fluid that you can get, and put the lid back on. Keep doing that until you have anywhere from a pint to a quart of herbal water.

Rose water made this way has a ton of uses; as most herbal waters are slightly acidic, they can be great astringents, and rose water is used as an ingredient in cooking and in making Lebanese tea. But for sorcerers, it has all the properties of the rose plant - and with alcohol (vodka or Everclear) added to it at four parts herbal water, one part alcohol, you can stabilize it and preserve it. It won't last all that long without the alcohol, and with it, bottled in a darker bottle and kept in a cool place, it'll last a good while, perhaps **3-6** months.

You may be wondering how these waters, oils, and tinctures can be used sorcerously. Simply put, they can be used to rinse and bathe other ingredients in workings to bestow certain influences on those ingredients - soaking a piece of clothing belonging to a man or woman you desire in rose water or adding a few drops of tincture to various dusts or powders before mixing them well and adding them to mojo-bags are just two examples. Seething these waters or waters with the tinctures added to them and steaming or hanging things over them (like mojo-bags, cloths, doll-babies, and the like) to implant influences into them is another example. Oils can be used to anoint or rub anything to give influence, including finished mojo-bags.

Waters and tinctures can be added to baths for various reasons, or used to make washes. They have countless uses, aside from possible medicinal use or even (sometimes) cooking. I make it a point to put aside those extracts and herbs and preparations that I'll use exclusively for sorcery, but perhaps that's being too inflexible at times. You need to keep an open mind.

An infusion is a preparation that nearly everyone knows - teas are infusions of herbs made with boiling water. Infusions are made (typically) from the delicate parts of plants, like the flowers, leaves, and green stems. One ounce of the dried herb or two ounces of the fresh herb are put into a non-metal container and covered with around two cups of water that has been boiled and then left to sit for thirty seconds. The container with the hot water and the herb is covered for five to ten minutes, and then the mixture is strained. It doesn't keep long, only a day or so.

A decoction is an infusion made of the tougher plant parts, and it is made the same way, though it is made in an enamel or stainless steel pot, with cold water put over the herb, and boiled for 15 minutes before straining. When used for medicinal purposes, the dose is a cup of either of these two or three times a day for adults, and half a cup two or three times a day for children under 12. These are sweetened just like tea - with honey and fresh lemon juice, or brown sugar - and usually sipped hot.

Oils used for sorcerous purposes in hoodoo are typically mixtures of more than just oils - pinches of blessed salts and powdered dried herbs are added to the base oils, as well as other objects and substances of power, which sit in the oil, adding their influence. Three kids of famous oil - Crossing Oil, Uncrossing Oil, and Van Van Oil, are well known to most practitioners. The truth behind these oils is that there are countless recipes for all of them, and each conjure man or woman will make their own.

Crossing oil is essentially one, two, or three actual infused or essential oils of plants that are traditionally associated with jinxing or hexing, combined with other baneful ingredients. Most good herbals will give a list of plants and substances associated with jinxing for you to create your own recipe out of. A typical and simple one (though no less powerful) would be to mix the infused oil of red pepper and peppercorns with a pinch of sulphur, a pinch of graveyard dust from a proper grave and properly paid for (described soon) and a pinch of powdered rattlesnake skin or bones, or some powdered dead and dried spiders, particularly of a poisonous variety. Some powder some of an eggshell from a black hen's egg and add it, too.

Anytime I say "a pinch", I mean in proportion to the container size - a vial of oil always takes a pinch, but a jar or larger bottle would take more in proportion. All oils should be shaken well before they are used.

Uncrossing oils are the inverse of crossing oils; they start based on oils of plants that are traditionally associated with cleansing and purification and un-jinxing or warding away curses and hexing. An oil of rue and angelica, or an oil of bay and ginger or rosemary, with a pinch of salt added to it, and some powdered High John and/or powdered garlic, makes a suitable "uncrosser". A few drops of ammonia can be added to it, as well. Sandalwood and patchouli essential oils can be added, in small amounts, to any uncrossing oil; and lastly, an oil of five-finger grass is always a help in these.

The famous Van Van oil needs a mention. Van Van is an old hoodoo oil, but I've heard that it can be made into incense, or powders, that can clear out evil, magically protect people or places, open the way to new opportunities, change one's luck for the better, and empower gris-gris or charms. It is also the oil used to anoint the famous lodestone that is so popular in hoodoo. Van van oil is so called because the Cajun and Creole French pronunciation of "vervain" is something like "vah-vahn." While I can hardly resist putting some oil of vervain into my Van Van oil, the real main oil constituent is lemon grass. Other citrus-like oils are good in it, and a pinch of salt into each dose made is good. Oils are used by me, primarily, to dress candles, which we will discuss soon.

After reading the essay before this one, it should be clear that in my conjury, the true "fire" of any oil, tincture, mixture, or preparation is the invisible force of the spiritual powers that I ally with, or of spirits that I coax into helping me, through the work of the House of Spirit. That is the hidden "other side" that gives these substances their true might.

V. Graveyard Dirt and Earth Charms

Graveyards, cemeteries, and all places of burial are powerful places.

The power of any field or stretch of land is already profound; to place the remains of the dead in the ground, and create places of memory and spirit-contact on top of the earth and within it, only adds to the power, exponentially increasing it. The soil of burial grounds is infused with the power of life in an intense manner - the sacred vessels of life decay in it, and something of the essence of the dead become resident in it. Burial sites become doorways of a kind, between the seen and the unseen.

Hoodoo is filled with references to the magical uses of graveyard dirt, dust, or earth; despite what some new-agers have tried to say, graveyard earth is precisely that - earth taken from graveyards in a certain manner, paid for in a certain way. It is not a "code name" for a powdered herb of any sort. Cemeteries and graveyards in the modern day have taken the place of the more ancient ancestral burial grounds that ancient cultures and societies often bonded with on a profound level - the sacred earth was not just the giver of life, but the taker of life and taker of the dead; the buried dead are merged with the ground physically and on the level of soul and spirit, integrated in a new manner, and they empower their burial sites and the ground as a whole.

Traditional spiritual beliefs from many places deal with the dreaded topic of "necromancy" more than most people realize. For most, "necromancy" is the art of divining the future from the spirits of the dead, but I use it here, as others have used it, to refer to any and all sorcerous workings that integrate the spirits of the dead or things relating to them. As the cults of the dead are so naturally combined with land-veneration, crop-cults, and other land and earth-based workings, it is not so odd to comprehend a "necromantic" element seeping through these ancient natural institutions.

The animistic-necromantic view takes one to deep places. When a body and a soul go to integrate with the land, and the spirit goes to take up residence in deeper, stranger places, the body of the living being eventually fades and rots, but the life-force (and spirit) diffuse and travel - all of nature broadly, but the land of interment especially, becomes the new "body" of the deceased, and all things that grow out of that land become new extensions of the dead. Animals and even people that depend on that land for life become new extensions of the dead. All is shrouded in a sacredness through transformation and integration. The soil itself is the medium of this transmission; swamp water or a lake's water can be the same if a dead person were to fall beneath it and decay there.

Graveyard earth becomes a powerful substance and symbol of two worlds overlapping. Work that requires the help of spirits generally, or of specific dead persons, can call for graveyard earth to be obtained. Graveyard earth is a major constituent of Goofer Dust, (Goofer coming from the African word "Kufwa", meaning "to kill") a very baneful substance used in many jinxes and hexes, but graveyard earth can be used for many workings with many different goals, even positive ones.

The ancient idea of the ancestral cult comes through strongest in hoodoo when we discuss the collecting and use of graveyard earth, and the metaphysics behind it - and the ancestors tend to be concerned with the well-being of their kin "above ground". The ritual of "hammering down", used to stake a claim to land and be prosperous on that land and in a home on that land, (which I will discuss soon) utilizes the blessings of ancestors obtained through graveyard earth.

You don't just go and take graveyard earth; you buy it. It is normally paid for with a silver dime, three copper pennies (pennies minted in 1981 or before) or a glass of rum or whiskey - sometimes just one of these things, or all three together, depending on what you have or what you feel inspired to give. It can't be taken without some sort of payment and then used with any effectiveness. The payment can be offered to the spirits of the entire graveyard, or to the spirit of the person whose grave you'll be taking dirt from, and this brings up another axis of understanding this process.

Before you can take earth from someone's grave, you have to do a minor form of spirit-talking which really boils down to asking politely for their help, and then really listening within to see how you immediately feel, or if you "hear" them communicate back within. Pay attention to your feelings on this point, and don't take something if you "hear" or feel that you shouldn't. Who lies in the grave is important, and where you take the dirt from is also important.

Of course, you always have to be respectful. But you have to consider what you want the earth for. Taking it from the graves of relatives is excellent and easier, as they loved you in life (in theory) so still probably want to help you in some way. But stranger dead persons can become "known" by you and you by them, if you spend time visiting them and giving gifts. Who they were and how they died matters. If you needed help getting a man to fall in love with you, and your mother (who passed away a few years before) always hoped to see you get married and have her grandkids, paying her for some graveyard earth and digging it from her heart-level is ideal; she'll certainly help, and this is a matter of emotional importance to her and you.

I've heard it said that grave dirt from the graves of soldiers is potent because in life they were strong people who had obedient spirits (taking orders a lot) and tended to be duty-oriented and honorable. You'd take from the head if you needed their knowledge or help with your own "mental" duties or tasks; you'd take from their feet if you needed their physical strength. I personally would take from the feet for curses, or possibly from the heart if the person in the grave shared some hatred with me for the target of the curse. Taking from the head was apparently also used for charms involving the gaining of money or wealth.

You can enter a graveyard where you know no one, and wait to "feel" where you are being led, to what grave and to whom, and try to gather from that grave, but I always feel it is best to know the persons from whom you are digging earth, at least somewhat - a little research can go a long way. A person who "died badly", i.e. a murder victim or someone who died tragically through a violent accident, is good for gathering graveyard dirt for cursing or jinxing.

But there is even another layer of detail here - a person wrongly executed can help you if you need justice, for the logic runs that they understand what it means to want justice and have trouble getting it. But at the same time, their spirits or even ghosts may have become bitter and malevolent, and they may seek vengeance against the people behind their deaths, or entire classes of people associated.

A black man, wrongly convicted and executed, may hate all white people (to make an example) if the entire prosecution team was white. A mother who had to lose all of her children to an epidemic sickness may now exist to try and help save as many sick children as possible. A friend or relative or stranger who died tragically in a car wreck while traveling may help you to be safe in travel with your family. These are all things to consider.

If you want simple, general graveyard earth, and if you understand that it isn't nearly as strong as properly discovered and taken earth, pay the entire cemetery and take some from the gates of the place. It's much weaker, but it serves its purpose. Graveyard dirt has an inseparable link to death, and one charm I've heard of requires a black candle, representing an enemy, to be turned upside down and snuffed out in graveyard earth, representing their death. More on candles soon.

"Hoodoo Herb and Root Magic" gives excellent examples of how graveyard earth can be used in tricks and conjuries. The authoress of that book points out that, generally, graveyard earth is used in causing death or unnatural illnesses or jinxes on enemies, for getting luck gambling or gaming, for protection, or in coercive love spells. One charm she lists requires a person to mix graveyard dirt and sulphur with an enemy's hair or some body part or fluid, and put the mixture into a bottle with **9** pins, **9** needles, and **9** nails, and bury it under the doorway or in a place where they walk, while the moon was waning, to cause them to hurt or waste away. This would be a saturnian work of extreme potency, and the bottle should be created on a Saturday night, and if possible, buried on a Saturday night.

Showing that graveyard dirt's use is not always baleful, she lists a charm (likely from Hyatt) that instructs a person to place graveyard dirt from the grave of their strongest ancestor around their door, or wear it in their shoe with salt and red pepper mixed in, to ward off jinxes. If the ghost of a young mother is harassing her children, taking some of her graveyard dirt to the home and laying it across the doorway will stop her - it has the power to render the ultimate lesson of change and mortality to the dead.

A good example of a coercive love spell, which is in essence a means of "goofering" someone into love, requires a man or woman to take dirt from a loved one's grave, from the heart level, and pay for it with a silver dime. Then, blending into the dirt a little powdered vandal root, sprinkle it secretly on the one they desire, while asking the spirit to help you. The source I got this spell from says that it has to be "kept up" to keep it going strong. A saturnian/venusian work like this should be done on Fridays.

One of Hyatt's collections gives the following charm utilizing graveyard earth:

1310. Ah hear about dat too an' ah knows of it. But chew have to pay three pennies but chew gotta go to someone's grave dat chew knows well. Jes' lak, yo' know, some of yore family dat's been buried an' yo' go to de head of dis grave an' yo' pay dat dead man or dat dead woman - whoevah yo' knows - de three cents. An' den yo' take some of de dirt an' den yo' tell dem to give yo' luck, don't let nobody harm yo', an' yo' bring dat graveyard dirt - git a bah'ful of de graveyard dirt an' bury it undah yore steps. Bury it undah yore step an' den nobody can't do yo' no harm cause de dead will pertec' yo'.

[Sumter, S.C., (**1348**), **2330:8.**]

One of my favorite aspects of the use of graveyard earth is the ritual of "nailing down" one's own claim and well-being on a piece of property that one has inherited or purchased. You can even do it if you're renting land and a home, though it is stronger if you're dealing with something more "yours". "Nailing down" is not just for protection, but to stop you from being forcefully evicted, or having your presence there forced away for any reason. You'll need four railroad spikes, one for each corner of the property, or four small nails if you're nailing yourself down in an apartment. Dress the spikes or nails with a peace-oil or a protection oil, and pray over them earnestly, asking that you be kept solidly and safely in this place "like a tree planted before water" - and that you not be moved.

Then, drive the spikes or nails into the corners of the property with a hammer. Put a silver dime on top of each spike, some graveyard earth taken from an ancestor or caring relative's grave, and then "set the spikes in place" by urinating on top of each of them - like a wolf marking territory. The addition of ancestral grave earth elevates this charm to the level of staking a claim on ancestral turf, of bonding with the land in which (in theory) you have loved ones buried in.

Earth doesn't have to be taken only from graveyards. Earth from banks, especially banks that are doing well in the current economic climate, is great for charms designed to get you money or financial stability. Earth from churches is great for protection from wicked or malevolent spirits. Earth from a courthouse is good for success at legal matters. A garden where fragrant, beautiful (and hopefully traditionally venusian) plants grow is wonderful for love charms. Earth from a hospital can be used to help heal the sick. Earth from a jail or prison is good for keeping the law away. If you need protection from enemies, earth from a police station is good. If you need a job, or money, or success in your business, earth from a busy, thriving marketplace is great.

VI. Sorcerous Methodologies

Now, to the topic of foot-track magic and other methodologies of sorcery. Anytime someone sinks a footprint into the ground, the earth within the print has some relationship to them personally. If you can obtain earth from someone's print, you gain a measure of sympathetic power over them. You always scrape the earth towards you, not away from you, and directly into the packet of paper or the little vial or bottle you'll be catching it in. You can use a knife, or some wooden instrument, but I try not to touch it with my bare flesh.

This foot-track earth can be used as though it were a material link to the person, and it makes a fine mixer-in with goofer dust. This sort of magic also deals with places that a person walks often, including their front door or back door, or a trail they like to jog on, or the like. Placing jinxing charms or any charm intended to affect them under a place where their feet touch the ground often is a powerful way of influencing them, and goofer dust, or the famous "hot foot powder" is sometimes scattered onto the bare earth, so that they'll step in it.

Sorcerous methodologies always follow this sort of "connectivity logic" - the serpent that entwines through all collects all, and everything that touches remains connected in a sense even after physical contact is broken. When you lay down dust of any kind, don't walk forward while doing it; walk backwards. This is a rule from tradition. How things are done, in what direction, at what time, in what manner - it all matters if you pay attention to the sympathy of things.

When you fold paper, with written requests on them or with people's names on them, if it's about something you want brought to you, fold it towards you, or alternatively, fold it clockwise. If you're trying to jinx it or get rid of the subject of the paper, fold it away from you or counterclockwise. Do whatever you're doing at dawn if it's about starting new; do it at dusk if you're trying to end something. Do it at midnight if you want something dead or jinxed. Most people consider the stabbing of doll-babies that are bound to an enemy with sharp objects like thorns, nails, needles, bird talons, or the like, to be the worst curse imaginable, but in truth, burying the doll-baby in a small coffin in a graveyard is the deadliest, carrying out a mock funeral.

Color matters. You want a guy? Write his name on a piece of brown paper, (like a paper bag) and write it nine times. Write it in pencil - all requests or commands that are written in pencil have more power because the lead "grounds" the request in its heavy power. Write your name over each of the nine, blending the names together, and fold the paper towards you three, five, seven, or nine times. If he's black or of dark complexion, put it in a bottle of dark syrup. If he's white or of light complexion, put it in a bottle of light syrup.

To those syrups, attraction or lust oils can be added, made from venusian herbs or other herbs associated with getting love. Graveyard earth from a helpful relative or friend can be added in pinches, if you paid for it and asked them to help get this love. You can keep the bottle in a certain place that has sympathy with attracting things to you - like by your front porch or under your porch or steps, under the door of your home. Do this on a waxing or full moon, a traditional time for increasing and gaining things. If you were me, spirits would be conjured to empower this charm.

Before I conclude this section, I thought I should mention something about numbers in hoodoo and sorcery. Threes and Nines have more than just the associations I gave them a few essays back; they are also odd numbers, and odd numbers are energetic numbers, dynamic numbers. They aren't stable, so they add power to things, get things moving. Even numbers are stable and square. Few people use them in charms that need a lot of power, but I am told that some prefer to use even numbers in curses, especially binding curses. That makes sense to me, but I'd go by intuition before any work.

When in doubt, you can't go wrong with three or nine, or with odd numbers, and that means that when you make preparations, charms or things like conjure-bags, or the like, try to make sure that the ingredients are numbered odd (or even if that's what you're going for). The simple love bottle charm above contains (let's say) paper, syrup, and graveyard dust. That's three. You can turn it to an even number by adding a pinch of blessed salt, or a strand of hair from the man you want (or woman if you were doing it for a woman.) You could turn it odd again by adding some venusian oil of some sort. It's very easy. I'm in the "odd" school, myself.

Nails are the last issue I need to cover. Nails have a long history in hoodoo and root work, and even though they are often used for hexing and the like, they can be used for other things. Nails have connections with the places they are used and where they remain for a long time. Finding a rusty old nail in the dirt of a graveyard is like finding a grand treasure - those old graveyard nails are impregnated with grave spiritual power, and can be used for the most baneful and deadly works imaginable. They go best in hexing bottles or war water (which we will discuss next).

Nails are a touch martial in nature, regardless, for they represent intruding force, and nails taken from certain places are, like earth taken from places, "tuned" into certain sorcerous acts. Nails from hospitals can help get enemies injured. Nails from courthouses can make someone have a bad day in court; nails from a jail can help to get someone arrested, and nails from a person's job site can help them get fired. Rusty nails and older nails are always worse, always more baneful.

When laying tricks, it is important to understand the importance of location and disposal of remains. Hoodoo is not a very abstract sorcery, and nor should it be. It is part of the world and part of people, and above all it is practical; it has a natural logic to go alongside its mystery. Putting a trick in a building - especially hiding it in the building, either while it is being constructed, or somewhere in it later - keeps the trick operating for the whole life of the building, and the trick is, of course, influenced by the nature of the building.

Dropping anything at a crossroads will disperse its power, but disposing of a trick by burying it (or its remains in the case of candles or burned or spent things, see below) in a graveyard sends its power to the spirit world and gives it a kick in effectiveness and strength. Burying or hiding a trick done to help you somehow, or you and your home situation in your actual yard or in your house is good; it keeps the influences operating right there in your living area. I have discussed dispersal of power before in my first essay in this work.

Hiding mojos or tricks in the clothes of a victim, so that they touch the flesh every time that person wears the clothes, is powerful; your own tricks or conjure-bags or the like made for your friends or yourself can be sewn into clothes or incorporated into clothing, so that they touch you all the time, but I'd hate to wash clothes with conjure-bags in them, as the water would alter it, no doubt, or destroy it.

Making people eat your conjury is another way of influencing them; putting powders or oils or waters or other preparations into their food or drink is both an ancient and powerful form of influence. Bodily fluids can be used directly as influence; women would put some of their menstrual blood into stews or gravies or other food to pass their power into men over whom they wanted influence, and men could do the same, using their own special additives. Burying tricks at the roots of trees is thought to disperse them, but hanging them from branches is a way of giving them a place to rest and spread their power.

Fecal matter, however, is never used for anything except the most horrid of curses (and rightly so). The modern addition of the toilet has given sorcerers an excellent way of flushing away things and powers they no longer desire to have in their lives; I have read that wiping an egg all over your body, and then breaking it in a toilet and flushing it is a good way of "flushing away" old psychic bonds or ties to others, and other un-cleanness. Writing an enemy's name on paper or putting their image onto paper, defecating on them in the toilet, and then flushing it, is a simple hex using feces. I have seen and heard of other, more complex hexes involving feces, and hope that I never have a use for them.

When I'm doing particularly baneful works, and I intend to gain the aid of spiritual helpers, I don't use sweetgrass to coax them into the materials; that tends to be counter-productive as sweetgrass is just a bit too kindly. But offering the powers liquors and wiping those onto the objects is better. Besides, blowing sweetgrass onto the bane-items might put some of my breath into them, and I wouldn't want my breath or any part of my life-force in objects that are going to get some awful treatment.

VII. Conjure Waters

Where you obtain water from is sorcerously influenced by similar laws to the obtaining of earth. Where water comes from, and sometimes when it comes, endows it with certain powers and influences: collect the water of the first spring rain (the first rain on or after March 21) and you'll have a water that should be bottled and used in renewal charms, in charms for maintaining youth, or purification, renewal, and cleansing for the house or renewal otherwise.

Water collected during a thunderstorm is "storm water" - one of the most potent talismanic waters in all of hoodoo. Storm water is a good basis for War Water, which we will discuss in a moment; but storm water, full of furious force, can be used to "wake up" mojo bags or conjure bags, or other charms, by sprinkling it on them. It "strengthens" pre-existing mojo or talismans, adds more power to them, or gets them "going" when they appear to have slowed down a bit.

You can sprinkle storm water around your house if you need a change, but I tend to be shy about that. Add brown sugar to it, and you can use it in money charms. Ocean water is great for both cleansing (it has salt in it) or for charms to help a woman conceive.

Moon water, water created by leaving a bowl out all night during a calm, clear full moon night, is good for washing the head and neck nine times over nine days to strengthen psychism. It's good water for deception or illusion charms. Washing the hair with it is said to encourage hair growth, but I think it's safe to say that something further needs to be added to the mix to get any luck on that front, but who knows? Enough odd things surround conjury to make me reserve judgment in most cases.

River water is potent for change, as it is full of dynamism. Stagnant water and water full of rot is good for cursing and killing or stopping something. Water melted off from snow, in my personal arsenal, is "freeze water" or "hindrance water" - used for influencing the stopping or binding of things. In my experience, nothing stops or hinders things like cold does.

There are three well-known "waters" in hoodoo, which deserve their own mention: war water, peace water, and Florida water. War water, as mentioned before, is a baneful water made to harm or kill foes. It is made with either storm water, or swampy, stagnant water, and then mixed with rust-dust, to make a reddish martial suspension, and to that is added some rusty nails, some graveyard dust or sulphur, and some Spanish moss, to help with that rot appearance and smell. You can further personalize it, by adding some of your foe's personal concerns (like hair or nails) to it, and the bottle of war water is used by hurling it at your foe's front steps or porch, shattering it, like some sort of evil psychic molotov cocktail, forcing your foe to walk over it or touch it, and blighting their home.

Peace water is precisely the opposite of war water, of course; it is used for bringing peace and spiritual cleansing to the home. It is made (in its basic form) of pure blessed spring water mixed with some Florida water, basil leaves, and some crushed eggshell. You add peace water to the mop water that will be used to mop the floors of the house, and wash the steps with it, and the windowsills and other major features of the house.

Florida water is a perfume or cologne water that can be purchased, even today, in drugstores all over the south and perhaps other parts of the country. It is a citrus-like, alcohol based cologne that was very popular in the first half of the last century, and it has dozens of uses in hoodoo. You can buy it on or offline, or make your own. There are many recipes; this is a famous recipe:

oil of bergamot 3 fluid ounces
oil of lavender 1 fluid ounce
oil of lemon 1 fluid ounce
oil of cloves 1 1/4 fluid drachms
oil of cinnamon 2 1/2 fluid drachms
oil of neroli 1/2 fluid drachms
essence of jasmine 6 fluid ounces
essence of musk 2 fluid ounces
alcohol 8 pints
rose water 1 pint

-- From "Fortunes in Formulas For Home, Farm, and Workshop" edited by Garner D. Hiscox, M.E. and Prof. T. O'Conner Sloane, A.B., A.M., Em., Ph.D. (The Norman B. Henley Publishing Company, 1937)

Florida water is most often used sorcerously for cleansing and purification purposes, but also as an offering to the dead.

Waters can be "robbed" from everyday items; an odd charm for "walnut water" has people boil 3 quarts of water with nine walnuts in it, until only one quart of brownish water remains. Put that in your bath, and bathe in it nine times, renouncing a former love or emotions you had - which you can't seem to get rid of - and then throw out the water at a crossroads or against a tree. Walnuts, apparently, have a traditional connection with destroying love-bonds.

VIII. Fires of Conjure

Burning candles for works of sorcery is as old as candles themselves. In the old days, no one had brightly colored candles; they used beeswax or tallow - natural wax or animal fat - and candles were either white, light brown, or darkish brown. Black candles were known, and so, legitimately speaking, white, brown, red, or black candles will serve you for any purpose. Of course, nothing stops you from using colored candles; planetary and sympathetic associations for colors are now well known and can be used.

Candles come in all sizes; the smallest I tend to use are votives. You still have enough room on those for carving names and sigils, or "waxing on" strands of hair or pushing finger or toenails into them, when you want to make a connection like that. Also, votives are the smallest candles that can be "dressed" with oil.

You should always dress candles, at least, with an oil created in sympathy with your work. I dress them in four different ways: I take the oil and rub it from the top of the candle to the bottom, if I want to attract something to me or someone else; I rub it from the bottom to the top if I want something to go away from me or someone else; I start in the middle and rub to the top, then go back to the middle and rub to the bottom if I want to separate two persons or powers; or, I start at the top and rub to the middle, then go to the bottom and rub to the middle, if I want to bring two powers or persons together.

It always helps to carve words or names onto candles, using needles or nails. I find that for longer statements of intention or longer names, it's better to use a word-sigil to carve the message on. You create a sigil by taking the phrase or name you want to work for or upon, and writing it on a piece of paper. Then, go trough the name or phrase and remove all redundant letters, and then take those letters and combine them into a sigil-symbol. The combined letters should make a finished sigil that cannot be "read" by looking at it, but your deep mind will know what it stands for, what it means.

If you want to make a sigil for a phrase outlining an outcome you wish for, don't ever use a phrase like "I want money" - all that will do is summon a condition in which you find yourself wanting money a lot. Instead, say "plenty of money" or something like that - use the present tense, as though what you had was there.

Carving someone's name (or your own) on a candle should be done three or nine times. The same goes with a name-sigil. The same goes with a phrase or phrase sigil; and again, direction matters. Carve them towards you if you're drawing towards you, or away if you're desiring to get rid of something. You can carve just one name, phrase or sigil if you're not working for any of those things, or just to "name" a candle after someone.

I like to put a piece of paper under the candle with the intention written on it, and let the candle burn down onto that. You always have to let the candle burn down all the way in one go if you can manage it; if not (if you're using a seven-day candle, for instance) then you can extinguish it and re-light it again later, but don't blow it out; snuff it out each time.

Above, I mentioned a hexing that had the sorcerer extinguish a black candle in graveyard earth to bring about someone's death; obviously, that candle should be carved with their name or a sigil of their name, and have (if possible) a picture of their face glued onto it, or parts of their body incorporated into it, somehow, for maximum effect.

The final "result" of a candle burning is as melted down bit of wax, and whatever you might have put under the candle, if anything. This needs to be disposed of in one of the usual manners - the remains have power.

IX. Uncrossing and Washing off Wickedness

Over time, dealing with other workers of sorcery or even spiritual non-human persons, you will get crossed or spiritually tainted somehow. Even doing baneful works of your own will drag you down, so I don't suggest you do those often. But there are countless - and I do mean countless - ways to cleanse yourself, uncross yourself, and to "wash away wickedness" or partially/totally remove the taint of wicked acts, which it might behoove you to know in your sorcerous career.

To begin with, purifying yourself is a matter of washing, largely. The simplest and easiest way is to put nine measures (pinches or palmfuls or other measurements) of blessed salt into hot bath water, and take nine baths over nine days in this water, collecting at least a gallon or so of it after you get out and throwing that token water onto a crossroads or against a tree somewhere. But many other methods are known. You can imagine what some of them must be like. One of my favorites is the use of nine egg whites; bathing in clean water that's had nine egg whites poured into it, and then sitting in the water as it drains out, cleanses you because the egg whites purify by grasping pollution and tugging it off you as the water pulls them off. Of course, you'd scrape up the dregs of that bath and toss them at a crossroads or onto a tree's roots.

When I say "bathe" in these formulas, I never mean with soap and shampoo and the like; I mean submerging your naked body, head, hair, and all, in a tub of hot water mingled with these ingredients, and using your hands to "scrub" every inch of you before being done.

One of Hyatt's formulas for "getting un-hoodooed" always stuck in my head, so I feel the need to repeat it now:

"If you think you are hoodooed, take one pint of salt, one pint of corn meal, one pint of your urine. Put that in a can on the stove at twelve o'clock at night and cook until it burns. Then throw the can and all away and your hoodoo spell will be off."

I've used this, and been impressed by its powerful effect.

It's important to recall that when you do baneful works - if you ever do them - you are not just causing a spiritual taint on yourself, but on the area in which you work. If you live with other people, try not to work in the house that you share with them. I go to a garage when I work banefully, because the last thing I want is my family to be affected by it. If I can help it, I leave my property altogether and go elsewhere.

If you must work in your home or on your property, you should use a cleansing mix of Florida water and/or peace water on the area, after you've cleansed yourself, and then (depending on the magnitude of the working) you may need to purify yourself again. The remains of baneful works should always be disposed of away from your house or property. Anoint your cleansed head and chest with some blessing oil.

Sometimes, you need extra-powerful personal cleansing, especially after bane works. A bath, or three baths, or nine baths of hot or cold water with an infusion or decoction of hyssop (or a tincture of the same) added to it is suggested. Hyssop is one of the prime (maybe THE prime) "cleansing off the sin" herbs. And, of course, wiping an egg over every part of your body and breaking it into a toilet and flushing it, or casting that egg into a crossroads or at a tree is also suggested. "Giving away the sin", using one or three copper pennies, held under the tongue as you walk to a crossroads is powerful; speak your wicked deeds as you walk, and when you reach the crossroads, spit the pennies - and the sins - out, and walk away without looking back.

A conjure-woman that I know described the hyssop bath in this way:

"The 51st Psalm is what you need for the hyssop bath. After you brew the herb in a pot or pan and let it cool down, you pour it into a tub of water. You can bathe in that, so long as the water isn't too hot in the tub. Or you can stand between two white candles, recite the

51st Psalm, and pour the cool hyssop-infusion over your head. After this cleansing, some people try to capture the dirty water and use it to wash their floors, especially if they done any kind of evil in a certain room. You can clean the windowsills and thresholds of the house to stop evil from coming in, too. When you're done with the water you used on yourself or your house, you gotta carry it down to a crossroads, and pour it out there. Walk away without looking back - bad spirits can follow you back if they see your eyes - and go home and light a good protective candle. That'll clean the sins off you and keep your place safe."

Your own imagination and sorcerous power can be utilized to devise more uncrossing and cleansing works. Those would be best for you.

X. Final Words

Now I have reached the end of this work on the basics of my conjury and hoodoo as I have known it and experienced it. There is still an enormous world of charms and occult lores out there, waiting to be found and learned and utilized. The purpose of this work was to help others to understand the highly personal nature of hoodoo-sorcery, and how tied to the simple substances and powers of life it really is. Sorcery in the most authentic sense is not something that you have to travel far to obtain, nor something that is so abstract as to be suited only to people who read Plato and Plotinus and do chants in Medieval Latin.

Sorcery is the "swirling force of the human being", the sum-total of our emotions and thoughts and feelings and our power to communicate, taken up to a level of wholeness and inter-connectedness. It comes to include substances and powers, times and places, and even elements, all in a web-work of force that swirls about and lashes out in line with our imaginations and will. It is the greatest of arts, the most satisfying taste of what being human really means, or at least it is to me.

I wish you all the best in your future works, your greater works that will take place long after you've moved past the starting points given here.

www.ingramcontent.com/pod-product-compliance
Lightning Source LLC
LaVergne TN
LVHW041340080426
835512LV00006B/550